D1601334

Learning-in-Community

Learning-in-Community

Reflections on Practice

by

Murali Venkatesh

Ruth V. Small

and

Janet Marsden

Syracuse University,
Syracuse, NY, U.S.A.

KLUWER ACADEMIC PUBLISHERS
DORDRECHT / BOSTON / LONDON

Library of Congress Cataloging-in-Publication Data

ISBN 1-4020-1387-6

Published by Kluwer Academic Publishers,
P.O. Box 17, 3300 AA Dordrecht, The Netherlands.

Sold and distributed in North, Central and South America
by Kluwer Academic Publishers,
101 Philip Drive, Norwell, MA 02061, U.S.A.

In all other countries, sold and distributed
by Kluwer Academic Publishers,
P.O. Box 322, 3300 AH Dordrecht, The Netherlands.

Printed on acid-free paper

Printed in the Netherlands.

DEDICATION

This book is dedicated to the memory of Jeffrey Katzer, wonderful colleague, friend, and early supporter of learning-in-community.

And to our many students.

On a more personal level, we'd like to dedicate this effort to Laila, Rahul & Ranjana (M.V.) and to Debbie, Jackie, and Dan (R.V.S.).

ACKNOWLEDGEMENTS

We wish to acknowledge the participation of non-profits in the Syracuse area. The experiences recounted here would not have been possible without their help. Thanks to Pam Heintz and Mary Anne Shaw -- service learning visionaries and pioneers at Syracuse University – for the inspiration. Thanks also to Dean Ray von Dran for the support extended to the ideas presented here over many years. And last but not least, the camera readying of the manuscript was aided immeasurably by Dong Hee Shin, Ph.D student at the School of Information Studies. Thanks!

And thanks to Sara Wason for sharing in our vision.

TABLE OF CONTENTS

CHAPTER 1

INTRODUCTION

This is a monograph on a particular approach to learning in professional education at the college level. We call this approach *learning-in-community*. To describe its most basic assumption in the simplest of terms, we believe that learners learn best when they take classroom learning out into the local community and apply it to real problems faced by real (organizational) clients; we term this active learning. Learners learn in many ways when they engage in such an experience. They learn by subjecting theories and principles to the real world. They learn through interaction with other learners like themselves who are engaged in the experience with them. They learn about the community they live in by working on its problems. *Learning-in-community* is not a new method, nor is it unique. However, looking back over the more than ten years that we have used it in our teaching, we can say that it changes both *what* is learned and *how* it is learned. It fundamentally changes the instructor's role. In this sense, it can be revolutionary in professional education.

In our instructional practice, we restrict the pool of clients to non-profit organizations. A small number of clients have been public institutions – government agencies, public schools, and public libraries. The rest have been community-based organizations – considerably smaller non-profits. Additionally, we restrict our focus to information and communication technologies (ICTs). Non-profits struggle daily with a host of challenges, and ICTs certainly are one of them. Most lack access to technical expertise and ICT resources, and CBOs tend to particularly poorly equipped in this regard. Our choice of client pool and problem domain was thus simple: we felt that we could help fill the knowledge gap to a certain extent through our classes, while simultaneously providing our students with active learning opportunities in the community.

As a method, learning-in-community involves small student teams, in the role of consultants, working closely with a non-profit client on their ICT problems. The first author began using the method in one of his upper level classes in 1991 at the School of Information Studies, Syracuse University. The decision to try the method was prompted by students. In their course evaluations from previous semesters, students had emphasized the value that "hands-on" learning might add to the course content, which was focused on telecommunications and computer networking. Subsequently, a faculty colleague helped identify a client site (a public high school). The first author developed a consulting exercise for use with the networking class in the 1991 Fall semester. The semester-long consulting experience offered through regularly scheduled, for-credit graduate and undergraduate-level classes today constitutes the core of our active learning model and has been used continuously by the first author since 1991. Our active learning model, presented in the following chapter, is an operational level description of the learning-in-community approach.

The first author established the Center for Active Learning in 1997 at the School to expand the range of technical services that could be offered to non-profit clients through the School's classes. Client evaluations suggested that while they found the consulting intervention useful, their needs often exceeded telecommunications and networking and included other areas – such as database and systems analysis, and user training. The Center was established to serve as a clearinghouse to meet these needs by matching them up with courses at the School. Relevant faculty were recruited to use their classes to address specialized needs of clients. However, with the growing indispensability of the Internet to non-profits, ICT networking has remained a staple client need throughout. Training the user on appropriate use of ICTs emerged as a vital new area under the second author's leadership. Again, the growth of the Internet and the increasingly important role that ICTs in general play in the life of non-profits has been a major impetus.

In 1998, a year after its establishment, the Center became part of a larger entity at the School – the Community & Information Technology Institute (CITI). CITI's objectives are broader than learning-in-community interventions and include prototype development and testing, and a research and development focus on the planning, design and implementation of advanced ICT solutions such as broadband. CAL continues as the main learning-in-community vehicle under CITI. CITI's service focus continues to be the non-profit sector in the local community. CITI's prototyping projects offer students additional opportunities for learning-in-community involving non-profit clients. Unlike with CAL projects, however, such opportunities are made available to students outside regular classes on account of the longer-than-a-semester duration of the average application prototyping cycle. Students interested in CITI projects undertake them as part of an independent study arrangement for credit.

Learning-in-community engages the learner actively in the content of learning[1]. The learner as *apprentice* must apply principles in practice, test their validity in that particular situation and modify as necessary, and demonstrate the suitability of the proposed solution to co-learners on the team, the instructor, and the client. The context could be simulated, as when the learner is placed in an artificial environment and asked to respond to stimuli there. Simulated contexts can be valuable tools for learning. A consulting case study, for example, may be designed to present a range of technical and social issues in a simulated organizational setting. However, actual work settings are usually richer and present the learner with a broader range of stimuli than would be possible with a case study. Importantly, the stimuli are "raw" in that the learner must process them. The learner must decide what the problem is before attempting to deal with it. Problem formulation, in other words, is a challenge

---

[1] Active learning has much in common with *experiential learning* – which is learning from direct experience and reflection. *Learning by doing* is another closely related approach.

that confronts the learner in actual work settings in a way that it cannot in a case study, however rich and ambiguous it is by design. Natural settings also allow client-centered effort, an important feature of learning in the professions. We believe that learning occurs in and through particular social configurations when learners work with other learners and relevant other actors in natural environments. Learning is thus *situated* in a multiple sense, with the consulting team's configuration (size, available skills, internal social climate) and its relations with the work setting contributing as much to learning as book principles. Learning arises as much from the learner's social participation in the experience as from technical skills mastery and cognitive operations. The content of learning – *what* is learned – and the social contexts in which learning occurs are intimately related.

2. LEARNING-IN-COMMUNITY: FOUR ELEMENTS

Learning for practice is an appropriate emphasis in professional education. Our program is founded on four elements: client-centered work in organizational work settings, apprenticeship, the social dimension of professional action, and project task design. The first three are enablers of learning and socialization in professional practice and may be influenced through the last. The instructor can design the learning stimulus – the project task – so as to influence the process and outcomes of learning for practice

2.1. Client-centered Work in Natural Settings

Providing a product or service to a client or clients is a hallmark of professional work (Schein & Kommers, 1972). The first challenge the professional often faces is locating the client. Who is the organizational sponsor and appropriate target of her effort and the recipient of its outputs? There is usually a related question that needs definition as well: Are there other, secondary clients? In our experience, learners tend to view the representative who functions as the liaison between the consulting team and the client as their client, at least initially. This person may well be a sponsor of the effort, but the person who decides whether or not to implement the team's recommendation may be someone else in the organization. In such cases, the primary client (i.e. the decision-maker) and the project liaison (who may be a secondary client) may have divergent views on the project's objectives. Should these differences be resolved and if, so, how should the project team resolve them? The project team must learn how to manage client expectations and client relations over the course of the project. Such functions form part of social maintenance functions (versus project task functions) (Hackman & Oldham, 1982) that an effective consultant learns never to discount. Project success depends on how well she manages task and maintenance demands.

Learners working collaboratively in teams also have *internal* clients. A team member is a client for a fellow member's outputs. The learner must manage task and social maintenance functions within the team, not just with the client(s) outside. Effective collaborative work depends on her ability to manage interdependence. An important aspect of this is her ability to learn from other members who may have different skills. Consulting projects often involve planning and design work; the client's problem is articulated and a solution is specified and recommended. The projects we assign our students require both. A learner may have skills in the first and not the second, while a second learner in the same team may be more proficient in design work than in planning. In this case, the first is a client of the second and vice versa. These learners must depend on each other to be effective as a team. Effective management of interdependencies calls for work coordination but depends equally on the social climate in the team. A learner's willingness to cross-learn will be affected by how conducive this climate is. Internal clients should get along; they should want to work together again in the future (Hackman and Oldham, 1980).

A defined client (or clients, as the case may be) is an important motivator of learning for practice. Once they locate the client, learners are working for him or her. The instructor, also a recipient of the team's outputs and therefore a client, becomes, relatively speaking, a secondary figure. The client on site becomes the cynosure of the team's work, not the instructor. The latter's role changes to one of facilitating the team's work of learning and performing so that they may satisfy the client.

2.2. Apprenticeship Learning Through Participation

Learning for practice may be thought of as apprenticeship. The apprentice learner is engaged in learning the ropes of professional practice, which spans not just task competencies but also social skills. Apprenticeship opportunities must support and encourage cross learning, so that the learner acquires (or, at a minimum, realizes her gaps in) necessary complementary skills. Structuring the project task into planning and design activities, for example, allows the learner to start in an area she is more familiar with and progressively learn in complementary areas by working with others. In the latter case, she would be a peripheral participant until she acquires the skills to move into a more central professional role in that area of proficiency (Lave, 1993). She learns by actively participating in the work along with peers with more expertise in that area, just as they might be active peripheral participants in an area that she knows better. This is a useful characterization of learning through apprenticeship in teams with heterogeneous skill sets. However, cross learning must be actively advocated by the instructor through the project task. It does not usually occur spontaneously.

Apprenticeship must include opportunities for socialization in the profession. The apprentice is not merely learning the necessary technical skills but also expects to become acquainted with the profession's ecology of practice – its norms and values, institutions, and active practitioners. This contributes to the apprentice's growing sense of identity as a professional (Lave and Wenger, 1991). Over the course of her project work, a learner may interact with a range of relevant actors on task-related issues. Her targets may include technology vendors and service providers (such as the telephone company or Internet access provider), professional consultants from area firms and university computing staff. She may contact geographically remote consultants over the Internet or telephone. Occasionally, alums of the course have served as informal consultants to student teams. Learning under such conditions tends to be viewed as meaningful for many reasons. The learner is actively engaged in real work (that is, work that has meaning and value for the client) even as she learns necessary skills. She is also being socialized into a community of practice through the actors she may seek out in connection with the task. Besides the professional self-identity she may develop through such contacts, interacting with practicing professionals helps to validate and ground concept learning in relevant ways.

2.3. The Social Context of Professional Action

As noted, our program is intended exclusively for non-profit organizational clients. With a few exceptions, most of our clients have been community-based organizations. CBOs typically are small in size (fewer than 25 employees) and provide predominantly social services in some of the neediest neighborhoods in a community. CBOs and the populations they serve form a section of the community that the typical college student is unlikely to come into contact with socially or as part of their education. We believe it is important that college students work in this sector. Their effort can help CBOs with an ongoing need (i.e. ICTs) while it acquaints them, through the project, with some of the community's social problems.

CBOs are the organizational have-nots of the Digital Divide. They are among the neediest when it comes to ICT resources. Few have adequate equipment and access to technical support resources. The CBOs in our community are no different, and it hampers their day-to-day operations. A $3.8 million advanced ICT-enabled community networking project was initiated in the late 1990's by a consortium of public institutions, CBOs and small business units in our community to bring social and economic benefits to the area (this project, which we refer to here as the Urban-net, is discussed in Chapter 3). CBOs realized early that they could not participate effectively in the network development process due to their lack of ICTs and technical knowledge resources. The advanced nature of the community network demanded both of would-be users. Ironically, the project was funded through a program aimed at improving non-profits' access to advanced ICTs. Learning-in-community programs like ours can help alleviate the knowledge resources problem in local CBOs if they can be sustained over time. The value to the learner lies in the realization that technical professionals can make a difference in socially responsible ways. College students tend to respond well to such opportunities in the curriculum. Many of ours have found working in the community highly motivating and personally rewarding.

As we argue in Chapter 6, the time may be opportune to develop a radical new view of practice. As ICTs continue to advance, the gap between the organizational haves and have-nots only grows wider and deeper. Already resource rich organizations are significantly better equipped to benefit from such advances. The disparities point to structural problems, which lie well beyond the reach of technically oriented interventions. Technical professionals interested in bridging this gap may have to start thinking of socially responsible action as including advocacy and representation of marginalized interests. This is admittedly a politically activist role. Urban planning practice appears to have developed along similar lines, starting out predominantly as an instrument of the state to its emphasis now on empowerment of structurally marginalized constituencies (Sandercock, 1998). The radicalized urban planner combines mastery of the technical aspects of planning with an activist social imagination. This can serve as a useful model for instructional programs that train socially aware ICT professionals. We outline some possible directions in the book's concluding chapter.

Professional educational programs attempt to combine intellectual rigor and practical relevance, with *relevance* usually referring to applicability: concepts learned in the classroom must be useful to *effective and ethical* practice. We believe that the notion must be expanded to include activist concern with the broader social context within which professional practice is embedded.

2.4. Project Task Design

The project task can be designed to influence the process and outcomes of learning. While it is the client's problem that provides the substantive focus of the team's efforts and its motivational charge, the project's appeal may be further enhanced through task design. Structuring the project into planning[2] and design[3] work highlights its skill variety and suggests division of responsibilities. Learners with analytic talents but limited technical skills feel valued when they realize they could lead the planning effort and assist technically proficient team members with design. Alternatively, technically skilled learners wishing to gain complementary skills could take the lead in planning.

Scheduling opportunities for regular feedback from the client, the instructor, and the class can be a motivator. Highlighting the socially meaningful nature of their work is not only motivating but is often creatively stimulating as well. A recent project involved the development of a local area network for a public library. The project site was in an immigrant-rich part of the community. In purely technical terms the project was only moderately challenging to the team. It became much more engaging when the students' found out that the client was interested in providing innovative services – free Internet access, Web use training – to the immigrant population. This realization triggered ideas on possible other uses and services, such as resume preparation and conversational English skills training via software. The project became technically more complex: how might the network be designed to best support the client's immediate needs as well as possible future uses? Its social significance greatly enhanced the project's motivational *and* intellectual appeal.

---

[2] Planning includes user needs analysis, and analysis of constraints and technological, technical support and other resources (e.g. budget) pertinent to the use site.

[3] Design refers to technical specification. Some of the projects involve implementing a solution proposed by a team from the previous semester. *Planning* and *design* in such cases refers to the implementation process.

Structuring the project is useful in a more practical way as well. Student teams are tentative at the outset. They are unsure that the project can be completed satisfactorily in the semester timeframe. Breaking it up into planning and design gives them a starting point. Planning work, however, can quickly become unstructured. Clients are vague about their needs, unrealistic about how urgently they need solutions, and what their latent constraints may be. They also tend to have a poor sense of what their technical support needs are likely to be when the solution is implemented. The scheduled feedback sessions are designed to sustain the momentum and help the team through the difficult early period in the project. The team's need to manage client relations is emphasized throughout the course but especially at the outset. A team that does this well usually finds that the planning process acquires more definition and becomes more productive when they better understand the client and vice versa.

Project task design occurs at two levels. At the top level, the instructor defines the assignment and through it, structures the project activity (planning and design) and clarifies its key deliverable (a consulting report to the client to facilitate informed choice and implementation) and its mechanics (formative reporting in class for feedback, for example). Problem setting or formulation occurs at the second level and is led by the student team responsible: What *is* the client's problem? Does it need to be bounded and if so, how? As they define the problem, the team is reminded to keep the means-ends question in view. Given a particular problem, what configuration of means would be needed to satisfy what ends? A faith-based coalition in the community used the resources of the class to develop an Internet-based free fax server. The coalition's officers (clergymen and women working in the inner-city) planned to use the fax service to quickly alert the coalition's members to emerging crises and problems in local neighborhoods. Given the circumstances, the means (i.e. the solution) would clearly have to satisfy stringent technical criteria such as high reliability and ease of operation. In addition, the social ends it would serve brought in other related criteria that the team had to think through carefully: Where should the fax server be located, and who would maintain it? How could the team ensure that the operator would have the needed skills to ensure reliable operation? Design concerns acquired new resonance and importance when the project's social goals were factored in. Problem formulation or setting can be directed so as to bring the social context of professional action into the learning enterprise.

3. LEARNING-IN-COMMUNITY AS PROTOTYPING

As an activity that unfolds in a social setting and through social processes of interaction between the learner and her peers and relevant others, and between her team and the client organization, learning-in-community is akin to prototyping. It relies on participation and communication.

The learner in such situations engages in a process of hypothesis generation and evaluation as she develops and progressively refines her ideas based on feedback from many sources: the client, her peers, relevant professional resource-persons, the instructor. The hypothesis testing process may be more or less formal and represents *epistemic* (Kruglanski, 1989, p.12) activity by which individuals make sense of new phenomena or situations. The term *hypotheses* refers to conceptualizations "embodying possible states of the world". During validation, hypotheses are evaluated on their relative plausibility with reference to some criterion. The process is assumed to continue until "some plausible hypothesis is advanced and supported by extant evidence" (Kruglanski, 1989, p. 14). The learner is an active inquirer operating in natural work settings rich with stimuli.

We use the term prototyping to emphasize participation and communication in learning. The learner offers representations – concrete or symbolic prototypes embodying hypothetical conceptualizations – of her emerging understanding and refines it or discards it based on the feedback she receives. By externalizing the representation, she facilitates participation and critique by others. Prototypes based on actual working systems can be particularly effective in directing the learner to take into account the particular context of use. Systems prototypes take time to develop, but certain projects call for a prototype. The Internet fax server project is a case in point. This prototype took three semesters to develop and involved as many generations of students. Not all of the projects in our program result in systems prototypes.

A systems prototype is a concrete mock-up. It is functionally incomplete by design and is meant to be iteratively and collaboratively refined in conjunction with the user. It invites responses from stakeholders by being concrete, and by contextualizing abstractions in a specific use environment. The fax server project serves as an example. The team realized early that they were not designing a fax server; they were designing a fax server for a particular client. In developing the prototype system, the team had to be mindful of the use context, which featured mongrel systems and no guarantee of ongoing technical support, an uncertain Internet connection and a minuscule budget for hardware and software upgrades. The prototype helped contextualize the design by prompting questions from coalition members on how the server will be used *day to day*. Such questions may not have been as probing without the prototype system. This mode of design – design by inquiry – continued after the prototype was developed and tested and helped both parties immeasurably. Schon (1983, p. 79) wrote of the designer thus: "He shapes the situation, in accordance with his initial appreciation of it, the situation talks back, and he responds to the situation's talk-back. In a good process of design, this conversation with the situation is reflective." The use of prototypes can facilitate "talk-back" and aid reflection by both learner and client.

Even when a systems prototype is not planned as part of the project, learners are directed to pay close attention to the use context – in particular the technical support available in-house – before recommending a solution. The social web of computing (Kling & Scacchi, 1982) – which includes technical support and software programs and technology budgets – is a critical enabler of organizational computing use. Design activity must reference the technological artifact as well as the environment in which it is embedded. This may seem obvious, but learners initially are much more interested in technology and much less so in the social environment. It is messy and frustrating. As the fax server project showed, prototypical depictions of the proposed system in a day-to-day use context can serve to clarify technical issues for the user and social issues for the developer.

4. TECHNICAL RATIONALITY VERSUS HOLISM IN PRACTICE

This book is based on practice and reflection. We have drawn from the many tens of projects that have been completed in our classes. As faculty responsible for these classes, our role has been that of facilitator or coach. We have worked closely with student teams, and with clients, vendors and service providers. This book is the reflective synthesis of our experience. The example below highlights the themes of learning-in-community: active learning in real organizational settings, the social dimension of professional action, and learning from reflection on direct experience.

The Urban-net[4] community network (mentioned earlier) was intended to connect public institutions, CBOs, and small business entities located in or providing services to residents in economically depressed zip code areas in the city. Network subscriptions were restricted to organizations (individuals were not eligible). Under the terms of the grant, subscribers were eligible for subsidized monthly charges and some support toward purchase of ICT equipment (called customer premise equipment). A major telephone company was tasked with developing the network's technology infrastructure.

Consistent with the aims of the funding program, the project proposal had envisaged using the network to deliver information and social services to the public, improve community cohesion by linking organizations across functional area sectors (i.e. linking K-12 schools not just to other schools but to the county department of social services as well), and contribute to the overall well-being of the city. Advanced technology would be used to advance the community's social and economic agenda. Desired uses of the network and its functional emphases had emerged from a detailed planning process conducted in the community prior to proposal development.

As noted earlier, the lack of ICTs and access to technical expertise made it difficult for CBOs to participate meaningfully in the design process (the small business units dropped out early in the process). Differences in interpretation of the Urban-net's function became apparent as well as the design process unfolded. The CBOs saw the Urban-net as a high-speed Internet access ramp. The Internet was an important resource and they wanted to be able to connect to it over high-speed broadband. Many were either not connected at all or wished to up- grade from dial-up modem connections. This was an urgent need, and the grant's subsidy made broadband affordable. The public institutions interpreted the network differently. They already had high-speed Internet access. Instead, they saw the network as an opportunity to meet their internal (i.e. intra-organizational) connectivity needs in a cost-effective way. For example, one large organization which provided technical support services to K-12 districts in three counties wished to use (a) the subsidized services to tie together the local area networks on its premises and (b) the network to

---

[4] Pseudonym, used here to protect the identities of those who were involved in the project

tie together the many school districts under its jurisdiction. Replacing its T-1 connections (T-1 is an older broadband technology) with a single subsidized connection via the grant was projected to save the organization many tens of hundreds of dollars annually.

Interestingly, during the planning process, there had been significant interest among community institutions in a range of network uses such as videoconferencing (for delivering telemedicine and other services), *one-stop* access to network resources through public facilities (e.g., kiosks located in the local shopping mall), an integrated database or information store offering a single-point of entry to all local data, and high-speed Internet access. The project's stated objective of promoting cross-sectoral connectivity would be advanced through such uses. However, interest in such uses (except for the last) diminished considerably when potential subscribers factored monthly service charges into their calculations of bandwidth need. With the exception of Internet access, the other projected uses would demand financial commitments from subscribers to develop and deploy. In contrast, using the project subsidy for internal connectivity or Internet access would actually save them money. Cutting subscriber's telecommunications charges, not the project's original social goals, became the overriding concern. Subscribers saw uses like videoconferencing as speculative and were, with very few exceptions, not yet ready to explore their use. They were understandably reluctant to contract for bandwidth for *non-priority* uses.

Divergence in connectivity needs raises urgent, moral questions for network design. Consider a user who only wants Internet access. This user's data are switched to the Internet access provider at the telephone company premises to establish the connection. A second user wants to access the community network for videoconferencing with a local organization. This user's data would have to be handled differently – with higher network performance assurances – because acceptable quality videoconferencing demands higher bandwidth connections. This user would be ill served if only the first kind of switching is supported by the network. The second kind of switching can satisfy both needs, but the monthly service charges may be higher all around, taxing the resource poor disproportionately. We use such examples to challenge students with value questions: How would they reconcile the issues raised by the needs divergence? What would they do to retain the project's original social goals while also meeting the CBOs' and public institutions' needs?

Design activity involves choices, and conflict is often a by-product of the design process. Conflict management is a key skill for the developer. Examples like the above underscore the potential for conflict in large-scale projects. Participant heterogeneity is a generally good thing in development work as it can foster creativity in design. However, with public projects like community network development heterogeneity can mean diverse social collectivities and institutions and contending interests and ideologies. The conflict potential from such a mix is high, higher than with projects undertaken within the confines of a single organization. Value debates were indeed prominent in the conflicts around the Urban-net project, centering on questions like *Whose network is it anyway?* and *What are appropriate uses of a community network?* Students training in the technical fields are not exposed adequately to value questions or conflicting situations[5]. Learning–in–community experiences provide learners many opportunities to reflect on such issues both directly, within the context of the consulting project, as well as indirectly through exposure to relevant other efforts in the proximate community.

The Urban-net project is a powerful argument for expanding the scope of design activity from technical specification to evaluating the consequences of technical choices in social terms. We refer to this expanded notion as holistic; design work is holistic in that it cannot be abstracted out of the social and historical context in which it is embedded and which it affects in intended and unintended ways. Holism complicates the designer's work and presents her with moral dilemmas; such dilemmas must be viewed as integrally a part of design work. A technical rationalist or instrumental view of design work is *acontextual*. The specific socio-historic circumstances of the design activity yield to purely technical considerations. In the Urban-net case, the telephone company was sincere in its concern that the project's social aims stayed in the picture through the design process. However, engineering and project management concerns took center-stage as the process unfolded, and the project's social goals weakened as overarching criteria for project success. Examples like this emphasize the need to understand design as essentially a value-laden activity. Design choices are not value-free but in fact benefit some social groups and interests over others. Advocacy to promote social responsibility in design therefore becomes a key antidote to such a bias. Whenever appropriate, the ICT designer should see herself as an advocate of broad social criteria as a measure of project success; equally, she should be concerned over the social ramifications of design choices. Holistic design would argue an activist stance. Given the growing dimensions of the gulf between the digitally rich and the digitally poor, learning-in-community initiatives programs should consider social activism to be a part and parcel of design training and practice.

Donald Schon (1983) observed: "From the perspective of technical rationality, professional practice is a process of problem-solving. But... we ignore problem-setting, the process by which we decide the decision to be made, the ends to be achieved, the means which may be chosen" (p. 39-40). Prompting learners to consider the ends served through design activity often also alerts them to the social context, and consequences, of professional action. It places the emphasis on problem setting, which is a values-based activity. From the viewpoint of holism, while the outcome of the design process might be a set of technical specifications, the design process itself often is, and needs to be, more than simply about technology. The holistic approach *combines* technical rationality and social awareness. Examples like the Urban-net demonstrate the necessity of the holistic design view.

There is renewed pressure for higher education to sensitize students to their civic responsibility. The work of pragmatist John Dewey is key to this interest. His argument that human capability has to be developed and placed in the service of

---

[5] "The issue of double and sometimes conflicting objectives is not directly handled in...system development literature and clearly needs more discussion among those practicing design" (Greenbaum & Halskov Madsen, 1993, p. 291).

what he called *social aims* has deeply influenced contemporary thinking on service learning in higher education. Dewey's ideas have shaped our learning- in-community effort.

Without taking away from the *intellectual* benefits that learning-in-community affords the learner, we can say that our students have engaged in and reflected on aspects of community life they may never have considered were it not for the project experience through our classes. By project-end many of them have felt that the experience was an eye-opener; many have also reported a sense of reward from serving the disadvantaged and the underserved.

5. PLAN OF THE BOOK

In Chapter 2 we develop an extended model of learning-in-community. Chapter 3 examines the *why* of learning-in-community initiatives: *Why do we need them? Why do we need them now?* The growing dimensions of the Digital Divide supply a major motivation for such programs. Advanced ICTs like broadband telecommunications threaten to exacerbate the gap and further marginalize the poor. We consider the *why* question in the context of ICT-based community networking and participation by community-based organizations, drawing on case studies (including the Urban-net) we have used in our teaching. The challenges faced by CBOs point to an organizational dimension of the Digital Divide, where some (corporate establishments and public institutions) are significantly better equipped with financial and knowledge resources to take advantage of new technologies than are others. CBOs provide services targeting the neediest residents in a community, so that their deprivation, in terms of access, is also that of their clientele. Learning-in-community programs can play a valuable ameliorative role with respect to the organizational gap by assisting CBOs with technical knowledge resources.

Chapter 4 presents findings from our evaluation of our learning-in-community program. Chapter 5 examines the *how* of a learning-in-community program. How does one set up such a program? We consider administrative, curricular and related issues, and discuss success factors. Chapter 6 concludes the book with a synopsis of the main concerns and a look ahead to *radical* practice in community.

CHAPTER 2

AN EXTENDED MODEL OF LEARNNING

1. INTRODUCTION

The youth center was located in the city's economically derelict south side. The center itself was precariously funded, barely hanging on to its faux-modern building in a seedy-looking lot on a tree-lined side street. Its director, however, was an energetic woman with ideas on the center's potential role in the neighborhood. She wanted to develop the center as a place where children from the neighborhood could come to learn basic computer skills – word processing, designing World Wide Web pages, online information search skills. This was good for character building and for discipline, she felt. Such skills would prepare "her kids" for jobs in the real world.

She had other ideas too. The neighborhood's (many) elderly residents felt isolated. Why not connect them to the Urban-net, an advanced ICT-enabled community network being developed in our community, through the center? They could talk to other seniors in the city's residence homes and exchange email and browse the Web over the Urban-net's Internet connection. They would be a part of the city in a way they were not at present. The network could connect the city's growing elder population and help enrich their lives.

The center's education room had a handful of very old personal computers. These were not connected to a local network or the Internet. The center's administrative computing infrastructure was modest as well. The technical staff, such as it was, was one person who "wore many hats" at the center. The receptionist helped out when she could.

This is one of many stories playing out on the shadowy margins of the digital revolution. Here's another.

The faith-based social agency had been established some years before and represented a coalition of over a dozen clerics from the Christian and Islamic faiths. Lay residents were also part of it, drawn by the possibility of using religious institutions and democratic means to improve social relations in the city's poorest sections. Fairly or unfairly, the city's poor felt victimized by the police. Periodically, they would get exercised over police action against a minority resident. The coalition would rally its members and other faithful in a church or mosque, meet with the Mayor and the police chief to press petitions, meet with the press, and, if the infraction was serious enough, organize a candlelight vigil later in the day in a public space downtown.

The coalition was headed by a pastor. He had obtained a donation of used personal computers and distributed them to several members of his board. A volunteer trained recipients on basic computer skills (this was apparently arduous: with a few exceptions, members were technophobes or slow learners). The plan was to connect all the machines to the Internet. The pastor used the telephone to get the word out to members on developments demanding the coalition's attention, but calling each member took time and effort.

Community-based organizations grapple with social issues at the grassroots but face significant barriers to ICT use. The youth center had outdated equipment they could not replace for financial reasons. The technical support available in-house was inadequate for realizing the director's dreams. The faith-based coalition had some donated equipment but depended on volunteer (and unreliable) technical support. They needed technical help to think through the problem vexing the pastor: how to mobilize the faithful without relying entirely on the telephone? The Digital Divide – the gap between individuals and households with ICTs and those without – is not as well known in its institutional form. But at the youth center and the coalition, the implications of the divide are real, urgent, in your face, and felt every day. Sadly enough, they are hardly atypical. Small entities like these have little in the way of technology and knowledge. They are often are critical components of a community's social infrastructure. If they are left out of the digital revolution, so are the populations they serve.

As it happened, the youth center and the coalition received help through our classes at the university. We were able to donate used personal computers to the youth center. Students enrolled in one of our classes then worked with the center's technical staff to connect the donated machines. The project was completed over two successive semesters, with two sets of student teams working on the problem. For the coalition, a student team proposed an Internet fax solution. All members of the coalition had a fax machine, and fax was easier to use than email. A team the following semester realized the solution, installing an Internet fax server (a computer that receives and sends fax out over the Internet) and demonstrating it live for the pastor (he was delighted). The software, obtained free over the Internet, could send out the pastor's message as an email message or as fax, depending on the recipient's preference. The team wrote a user's manual as well as part of their project.

The help we provide through our classes only highlights for us the enormity of the problem. Agency A has no computers. Agency B has a few but has no network; its director's husband had started wiring the place up in his spare time but the job was not completed. The wiring plant was undocumented, which meant no one except the husband knew which wire went where. Agency C, a community arts group, has this vision of digitally capturing and transmitting community arts programming to a community center over a network but doesn't know how. The list goes on and on. CBOs are severely challenged. The larger institutions, such as public hospitals and K-12 schools, are better off with respect to common office technologies but are under resourced when it comes to *emerging* technologies and applications. The need for technology and knowledge resources is deep, varied and significant in scope in our community institutions.

Based on our experience, we can say that learning-in-community programs can help with the knowledge problem. Such programs can offer a local, sustainable way to assist needy institutions. They can help infuse professional education with social values. We believe the following to be important if such programs are to thrive:

- The learning experience has to be offered as part of the regular curriculum, through regularly offered, for credit courses. Organizations should be able to count on help on a continuing basis if needed. Students lose interest if the experience cannot count toward their academic program. Being included in the regular academic curriculum is an endorsement from the school: it signals the learning as valued, relevant.
- Learning-in-community programs have to be prepared to offer help in a range of subject areas. A client may need help with computer networking one semester and systems analysis and database the next. Similarly, students should have an opportunity to work in diverse subject areas through different classes as they go through the program.
- Such programs should have access to technical resources to allow hands-on learning by students and clients. Learners' ability to test hardware and design and develop software applications (we refer to the latter as prototyping) depends on access to a technology lab or resource center. The resources may range from common office ICTs (computer hardware and software and local area networking gear) to more advanced technologies.
- The learning stimulus has to be carefully thought through and continuously refined. As it stands now, the stimulus we use structures the learning experience in terms of planning and design elements and fosters student peer learning. The client is often a co-learner with the student; the instructor becomes a guide and a coach. The motivating properties of the learning stimulus for the student are as important as the social benefit produced through it for the client

2. MICRO AND MACRO-SOCIAL RELEVANCE

Computing is a social technology. A particular configuration of ICTs is the result of social and political choices, and the designed product is better equipped to satisfy some users and needs than it is to satisfy others. The political and economic interests of powerful players shape such choices. ICTs can be used to consolidate the status quo or challenge it. It can bestow power or take it away. Technology choices have profound social implications at two levels. First, ICT planners and designers have to consider solutions within the context of the work practices, culture and power in the adopter organization. We call such an awareness the micro-social level of relevance in professional education. Learning that is relevant in this sense involves understanding the context within which ICTs are embedded and within which it is used. Attempts at changing the context have to start with a good appreciation of it; technical knowledge alone is not enough. Technology choices often do have many unintended consequences for the adopting organization. Contextualized learning confronts the learner with basic questions about the nature of technical professional practice: What is a consultant's role in the client organization? Who is the client? How can I be an effective agent of change in this milieu? The following example illustrates the urgency of such questions.

Some years ago, the recently appointed administrative manager of a local government agency wanted to change the computing environment in his office. He was enthusiastic about his new job and had ideas for improving the responsiveness of his staff to requests for information from the district attorney and the public. His office was served by a large, old mainframe computer located in the county offices nearby. He wanted our students to help him move to a local area network with personal computer (PC) workstations and servers connected to it. Under this new arrangement, his staff of 30 would not have to work with the mainframe directly; they would connect to it over the local area network.

The manager and his staff hated the mainframe. It was not easy to use. The technical staff that ministered to it was indifferent to user needs. It was not uncommon for them to take many hours, sometimes even a day or two, to generate a report for the district attorney on, say, criminal incidents in a certain part of the city over a certain period of time. The manager believed that with the new system his staff could respond faster to informational requests. He would control the system not the mainframe "techies", who he characterized as an aloof priesthood – an unresponsive entity answerable to no one. He needed advise from the class on technical design specifications for the local area network system and on connecting to the mainframe for access to public, non-confidential data. He had approached the techies for assistance in the matter but they had not responded.

The student consultant team that picked the project was warmly welcomed by the manager and his staff but met with hostile resistance from the techies. They had no use for the PC and could not or would not support PC connectivity to the mainframe on account of "security" concerns. They were unwilling to consider that only a small part of the information stored on the mainframe – non-confidential information in the public domain, like crime statistics – would be accessed by the manager and his staff over the local area network.

Despite the frustrations, the student consulting team came up with a set of technical design specifications for the network. But the techies were unyielding on the database access, refusing to meet with the students or share any information about the mainframe or the database. This even after the manager had complained to the agency head about the techies' attitude.

The students did not understand the situation until one of them asked to see the organization chart for the county. They soon realized that techy group had countywide responsibilities, were administratively under the county executive, and that the manager's agency, as a relatively small operation, merited only a small portion of their professional responsibility. They were supported as part of the county executive's overhead expenses and had no incentive to be responsive to the manager. They had not impeded the students' local area network design exercise, rationalizing it as an isolated experiment, but had strenuously fought the connection to the mainframe because they feared the PC. They feared losing control over the database. The PC was an instrument of subversion. The students learned a lesson on change agentry and organizational structure and politics that no case study, however rich and true as a simulation, could have brought home to them quite so vividly.

3. MACRO-SOCIAL RELEVANCE

Second, the *well-tempered* consultant is one who is sensitive to the implications of technology choices for society at large. The development of the Urban-net brought up many difficult questions at the macro-social level of relevance. Here are two examples:

- Aurora, a community non-profit providing sign language services to hearing-impaired residents saw video-based signing over the Urban-net as a way to improve coverage without increasing their staff of specialist sign language interpreters. Interpreters currently wasted a lot of time driving from place to place where their services were needed. Using video-conferencing over the Urban-net, they could provide their services at remote locations without having to drive there.
- However, would the Urban-net design be open to supporting such pro-social uses? Would its (big) politics and economics register the needs of a small, resource-poor non-profit agency? If it does not, how relevant is the Urban-net to certain sections of the community? These questions are being debated at this writing.

We emphasize both levels of awareness in our instructional practice. Both the micro and macro-social are constitutive aspects of relevance in our use of the term in this book. In this chapter, we discuss micro-social relevance and present an extended model of learning that requires learners to take this into account in their learning. The macro-social is considered in the next chapter and in Chapter 6, under the rubric of radical, transformative professional practice.

4. ACTIVE LEARNING THEORIES

There are two broad types of experiential learning: prior learning (knowledge and experience gained outside the learning situation) and sponsored learning – knowledge and experience gained through the learning situation, planned and supervised by the instructor but occurring outside the classroom. Theories of experiential learning tend to focus on sponsored learning. The basic tenet of sponsored learning is that learners learn best when they are actively and directly in touch with what is being learned. This is learning in the concrete, as a complement to learning in the abstract. Some form of associated reflection on the learning experience (during the experience) is usually a part of such learning. Learning-by-doing is a related term. Another related term, *transparent training*, refers to the learning of foundational principles when the learner applies those principles to solve a problem. That is, the principles are learned in the process of actually using them in practical ways.

There are two types of sponsored learning: synthetic and natural. The synthetic approach relies on case studies and other strategies, such as role playing, to simulate the context and entrain learning by doing. The learner is asked to imagine herself in a particular situation. The stimulus might read like this: You have just been recruited to lead *Out Of The Box*, a maker of innovative products that has fallen on hard times. Your charge is to turn the company around. How would you do it? Why would you do it that way? The learner has to specify action steps and defend them, in the process applying, modifying and perhaps even going against book learning as the situation demands. Natural sponsored learning, on the other hand, links theory and practice more directly by immersing the learner in the actual milieu itself. The learner learns in the natural setting, with all its richness and attendant complexities. The synthetic variant has its uses and we do use it in our classes. But we believe that sponsored learning under natural conditions adds value to learning in unique and powerful ways. Our focus is on natural sponsored learning; we refer to it, simply, as active learning in this book. We briefly review below some useful prior views on active learning.

The pragmatist philosopher John Dewey is a pioneering and influential figure in active learning. Dewey saw learners as apprentices. Just as painters learned by painting, learners in the professions, he believed, ought to learn by practicing their profession. Practice was critical for Dewey. Dewey believed there was "no such thing as genuine knowledge and fruitful understanding except as the offspring of *doing*. Thinking and doing are inseparable: Only by wrestling with the conditions of the problem at first hand, seeking and finding his own way out, does he (the learner) think" (Cited in Coyne 1995, p. 40).

Dewey argued that learning-by-doing prompted, invited, the learner to continually test book principles against reality. How did those principles transfer from the page to life? Learning becomes more immediate and less abstract when it is tested in this way, when learners are encouraged to ask questions about the world. It is important, as he wrote in another context, to learn through situations that offered opportunities for "continual training of observation, of ingenuity, constructive imagination, of logical thought, and of the sense of reality acquired through first-hand contact with actualities". The process of evaluation and testing is iterative: the test leading to action and new knowledge, the evaluation of that knowledge leading to a further test and so on. Such a cycle is key to Dewey's notion of balance: balance between knowledge and action, principles and practice, the abstract and the concrete, the inside and the outside, the person and the environment. Interaction between the learner and the environment personalizes learning, making it relevant, vital, and first-hand.

The social dimension of education is central to Dewey's conception of an engaged citizen. Knowing, he believed, should be linked to action. In *The Public and its Problems* (Dewey, 1927), he is concerned about the future of democracy in the age of machines, when civic engagement may weaken. His recommendation is the fostering of "the vital, steady and deep relationships" (Dewey, 1916, p.98) that characterize a community of fully engaged citizens. Education must free "individual capacity in a progressive growth directed at social aims." His emphasis on civic responsibility of public education is foundational to service learning. It is this civic dimension that differentiates service learning from other modes of active learning. Service learning provides opportunities for students to engage in service in a community as an integrated part of a course of study. Increasingly, this civic dimension is vital to professional education. Professionals must be engaged citizens first. The implications of this stance for social activism in the professions are explored later in the book.

Lewin (1951)'s and Piaget (1970)'s approaches to learning are similar to Dewey's. The Lewinian model emphasizes direct, immediate, concrete experience as the foundation for testing and validating abstract concepts. In addition, Lewin recognizes the importance of feedback in learner assessment. The Lewinian learner not only tests formal concepts against personal experience but simultaneously assesses her own performance against learning goals. Learning involves an iterative sequence of steps taken to reach a goal; the learner evaluates the outcome of each step before going on to the next. Recalling Dewey's notion of balance, Piaget viewed learning as resulting from the learner's interaction with the environment. Learning involves the effort of fitting new learning to experience (accommodation) and new experience to existing frames (assimilation). When the two processes are balanced, productive learning occurs. All three thinkers – Dewey, Lewin, Piaget, – view learning as a continuous process driven by direct engagement of that which is learned; the learner is seen as an active and adaptive inquirer.

The contemporary theorist Kolb (1984) sees experiential learning as a process that links education, work, and the learner's personal development. Knowledge is created through the *transformation of experience*. Learning occurs through a progressive cycle: direct experience, reflective observation, conceptualization, and active experimentation. In the experience stage, the learner is actively engaged in a learning event. She questions, considers, sorts out, clarifies, and classifies what she observes from the experience. The observations are subsequently transformed into concepts or reflections that are held in the mind for future application. In the fourth stage – active experimentation – she draws on this store when engaging a new stimulus, thus setting off a new cycle of learning. Learning involves working through the four-stage cycle. An instructor may be needed to guide the learner through the stages of the cycle.

Kolb neglects the social context of learning. Learning is social, situated, and occurs through participation in actual practice (Lave, 1993). The learner is an apprentice. She learns through practice and by interacting with other apprentice practitioners like herself. As apprentice practitioners, learners learn by doing and by engaging in the social interactions and relations that constitute participation. The physical context of practice allows her to test book knowledge *in the real world* and make modifications as suggested by what she observes. The social context of practice provides opportunities for instruction in socialization into the profession – values such as professionalism and reliability, commitment to the client and the task at hand, the importance of cooperation. Dewey himself believed that learning was situated: experience occurs through situations. The term *situation* refers to the interactions between the individual (or the group) and the "physical and social environment", and these interactions are central to learning. His approach has been called "relativistic: no human phenomenon can be considered without its general physical and social environment...Situation and interaction are Dewey's keywords..." (Findeli, 1995, p. 39).

Sponsored learning can occur anywhere: in the laboratory, where the learner learns in a synthetic setting, and out in the real world, in the natural context of actual practice. In our opinion, natural settings provide a far richer environment for learning and reflective action than do synthetic settings. They highlight the social context of technical work: technology solutions are designed and developed through a social process involving users and designers; it occurs in a social setting. Natural settings also highlight the social agreements or contracts under which such work is accomplished. Users and designers are mutually dependent. Design group members depend on each other to complete tasks. In the example described earlier, the student team had to be sensitive to issues not encountered in quite the same way in synthetic settings. They had to work with the primary client – the administrative officer – to define the scope of the project; the project scope had to be redefined due to opposition from the techies. They had to manage the client's expectation of what they could realistically accomplish in the project. They had to manage relations with the techies and the course instructor. As part of a self-managing task force, team members also had to manage relations with one another and keep an eye on deadlines and deliverables, while watching out for slackers or control freaks. They had to work with differing skill levels in the team. Such factors – some of which operate from within the team and others from outside the team – stem from the naturally situated learning experience and shape the team's work processes and outcomes. .

Constructionism offers a parallel view. Constructionism (or constructivism, a related idea) draws on Piaget to emphasize the active processes a learner goes through when accommodating new information into extant cognitive structures or frames. The building of *external* constructions is assumed to clarify learning and the fit between new ideas and received knowledge. Rather than viewing the learner "as one who just builds… cognitive structures while learning, constructionist learning includes building external constructions that engage the environment and give the learner feedback with which to reinterpret the experience" (Shaw & Shaw, 1999, p. 319). These constructions are shareable with others and could take many forms: "a sand castle, a machine, a computer program, a book"(Papert, 1990, p.3). The construction of new knowledge is believed to be particularly effective when such external constructions are personally meaningful to the learner. Learning is viewed as an active process, and the learner as actively constructing new knowledge drawing on personal experience. Constructionism emphasizes design and the act of making: the learner is believed to *make* new ideas, not passively *get* them.

A variant, called social constructionism, emphasizes the social setting in which learning occurs. It takes constructionism outside the physical classroom and schoolhouse. Recalling sponsored learning in natural situations, social constructionism focuses on the "construction of activities, projects, and relationships that help define an evolving community. Through this lens, the members of the community serve as active agents in the construction of outcomes and activities that produce a developmental cycle in the social setting" (Shaw, 1999, p.321).

Our model draws on many of these approaches. We view the learner as an active inquirer, one who actively engages the process leading to new knowledge. Learning occurs in the interaction between the learner and the natural setting of the sponsored learning encounter. Consistent with the view that learning is a situated activity, we believe learning stems from the learner's interaction both with the physical and social aspects of the natural setting. We see the learner as an apprentice who learns by doing – that is, by participating in actual practice and reflecting on the experience. Consistent with constructionism and its social variant, we believe that the construction of artifacts – or prototypes – is an important enabler of learning. The making of artifacts externalizes the learner's thinking, in the process inviting participation and critique from others in the environment. It makes learning a social, participative activity. When the activity occurs outside the classroom, it draws the broader community into the learning activity. As well, it exposes the learner to the physical and social realities of life outside the classroom. Our active learning model, presented below, is an operational level description of the learning-in-community approach.

The terms active learning and experiential learning are used interchangeably in the literature to refer to the reliance on direct experience to instruct students in applying methods and theories learned in the classroom. We prefer the term active learning and use it here to refer to sponsored learning under natural conditions or situations. Active learning is the broader term and subsumes experiential learning. It stresses the learner's active involvement in what is being learned. We have developed an analytic model based on research and practice in active learning. Over the years that we have used the learning-in-community method in our teaching, this still-evolving model has stimulated inquiry into the social context of learning (the arrangements and conditions that promote learning), and inputs and processes (the learning stimulus, the learner's motivation, the instructor's role and planned interventions). We present the model below and examine its central principles that, in our experience, promote learning. The model is not definitive but suggestive.

5. ACTIVE LEARNING: THE FIELD PROJECT ASSIGNMENT

The field project assignment has served as the active learning stimulus in our teaching. We have used this stimulus in our classes continuously since Fall 991. The assignment has been refined over the years, and has been used with over a thousand undergraduate and graduate students enrolled in the School of Information Studies and other schools and colleges in Syracuse University. Our classes have provided technical consulting and training services in information and communication technologies to over seventy-five public institutions in the local community, including government agencies, healthcare agencies, K-12 schools, and smaller CBOs. The bulk of our clients have been CBOs, because they are generally the neediest when it comes to technology. All services are provided free to clients.

A few weeks before the scheduled start of the semester, we send out request for projects solicitations to public institutions in the community. Occasionally, we have "adopted" one institution as the site for all projects that semester. More typically, the RFP solicitation yields a set of four or five sites each semester. The instructor then works with the client to define a slate of project topics; projects have to be technically feasible and should be such that a student team can complete its consulting work over the course of one semester (14 or 15 weeks long).

The projects start with a brief presentation by the client in class about a month into the semester. The client describes their need(s), and may touch on available resources and relevant constraints as well. Some clients prepare a one-page handout for the students. Students pick the project they want to work on. If, say, two teams pick the same topic, the instructor may persuade one of them to pick a different topic, but the team's interest is in a project is key and no forced assignments are made by the instructor. We strongly believe that the team has to be motivated in order to perform well, and interest in the topic is a strong motivator of high performance. The assignment accounts for up to 40 per cent of the course grade.

From this point on, the student team is fully responsible for directly managing relations with the client: the team coordinates site visits and other contact, schedules briefing sessions for the client on project progress, represents the client in contacts with vendors and service providers and interfaces with entities (individuals, institutions) within and outside the client organization on project matters if needed. The team is also fully responsible for managing its own task and interpersonal affairs.

Teams turn in two one-page progress reports during the semester. Up to thirty minutes per class meeting may be devoted to project-related discussions; students are encouraged to meet with the instructor outside class if needed to discuss project progress. Teams present their final report at the last two class meetings. It is a formal presentation to the client and the class. Clients are formally invited to attend by their consultant team(s). Presentations are followed by questions. Clients typically ask a lot of questions of the team and take extensive notes; many volunteer their assessment of the value of the team's work to their organization. Teams turn in two hard copies of the final report a week after the end of the semester. The quality of the planning documentation and the justification of the recommended solution are the primary criteria used in grading the final report. The client's evaluation may also be factored in.

While most projects conclude at semester end, some take several semesters to complete. These tend to be more comprehensive in scope, covering planning, design and implementation. The semester-long projects tend to be limited to planning and design exercises. The longer projects involve "generations" of students over several semesters. Such projects, while providing continuity of coverage, demand more coordination work of the instructor and the client.

If the project involves hands-on work (e.g., implementing a network), the team starts out by analyzing the client's requirements (needs), constraints and resources, and conclude by documenting the implementation work, the problems faced and lessons learned. Satisfactory implementation and the quality of the documentation are the criteria used in grading the final report.

5.1. Planning

The consulting assignment has two parts to it: *planning* and *design*.

Planning includes client requirements analysis, and analysis of the available ICT and human support resources and relevant constraints (e.g., financial constraints).

The focus of the effort is on collecting documented information as well as uncovering (or discovering) new information that may be less defined and less formal in nature. Archival technical documentation is a useful source of information on the types of computing and telecommunications infrastructure available at the client site. However, despite its obvious value, only a third of our clients have such documentation readily available. In the majority of the cases, student teams develop or significantly update such documents as part of planning. As an example of less structured data, the prevailing organizational culture vis-à-vis technology is unlikely to be spelled out in a formal way may nonetheless be a significant constraint on technological change. Localized knowledge of this type has to be uncovered, documented and actively used during design for the project to be effective. The planning effort tends to be open (in terms of structure) and time-consuming for these reasons. Students rely primarily on site visits, surveys and face-to-face meetings with the client and users to collect planning data. A team may make three to four visits over the course of the semester. We expect students to develop a good, richly detailed grasp of the client's requirements and organizational context through planning.

Planning also provides the criteria the team would use to assess the goodness of fit of the solution proposed through the design activity. Planning entails defining the problem and specifying the requirements that the solution must have (Schon, 1983). These criteria could be formal or informal, and could stem from financial, cultural or infrastructural considerations. A client site may not have the technological and human infrastructure to support the latest and greatest solution out there. Instead, the team's task is to recommend what is most *appropriate* for the client as judged by a well-developed understanding of client needs, available resources and relevant constraints. There is software that is available for free (e.g., Linux, an operating system that competes against Microsoft Windows), but at-hand technical support is often required to install *freeware* and keep it running. Many of our clients have little by way of technical support, and a freeware solution will not work for them. Solutions that call for user sophistication may not work either, for similar reasons. The criteria, crucial as they are for the learner's work, typically do not emerge naturally from interactions with the client or work at the site. Clients are notorious for not knowing what they want; learners have to work hard and closely with the client onsite to discover needs and wants, resources and constraints and to derive meaningful criteria from the mix. A well-executed planning effort usually underscores to learners the need to consider both social and technological factors in their design.

Planning entails what Donald Schon called *problem setting*. It is "the process by which we decide the decision to be made, the ends to be achieved, the means which may be chosen" (Schon, 1983, p. 40). Given the clientele we serve through our classes, broad social issues often impinge on the determination of the ends served and the means used. For example, in the case of Aurora earlier, the students could work up a technically feasible design for the electronic delivery of signing. But, considering that the Urban-net was not yet ready for such uses, what good would that do? A better strategy probably might be to broaden the design to include ways to educate (through prototypes and exemplars) the Urban-net leadership and the public at large on the pro-social possibilities of community networks. What, in fact, are the ends to be served, the decision to be made here? Clearly, it is much more than the design of a technical solution. It is the design of an intervention to highlight the opportunity for social good from community networks. These are *value* questions that reflect moral concerns, stemming as they do from questions of human welfare. Interestingly, in this case, questions of value may also be the pragmatic ones to ask. A purely technical specification for electronic signing would have little chance of realization on the Urban-net, given the prevailing climate of bottom-line thinking. On the other hand, an intervention carefully designed to raise public awareness around pro-social use of the community network might help build needed momentum in the community for such uses. College-level training and education programs in technical practice are seldom concerned with activist strategies defined around pro-social values or moral considerations. We believe it is important that this change: technical practice and social activism should be viewed as complementary. We expand on this in Chapter 6, drawing on the example of urban planning.

Confronting organization conditions *in situ* is a novel experience for many of our students. Learning under such conditions – which is dilemma-driven and marked by ambiguity and creative frustration – can be very stimulating. But planning is also often frustrating, our students have told us. The client's requirements are often poorly defined, ambiguous and plastic. It is a shifting, changeable terrain most learners encounter for the first time through the project experience. Most are unfamiliar with the larger social issues that impinge on their work at the client site. A good number of our clients are community-based organizations that serve marginalized groups in the community – the economically poor, the elderly, minorities. The consulting project is often the vehicle through which our students get their first glimpse of the economic and social challenges in the community. Admittedly, the class is about technology applications not sociology, and the project assignment does not require students to grapple with the social issues per se. We sensitize them to the issues and advice them of their relevance to design work, but the social issues themselves are not analyzed in class. But exposure to such issues sensitizes learners for the socio-technical nature of effective design work, and argues against the adequacy of a purely technical rational view of professional practice (Schon, 1983).

Learners should be discouraged from viewing planning and design as strictly sequential activities. Users' ideas about their own requirements may change when technical specifications are being discussed, that is, during design activity. Users may already have a solution in mind at the start of the planning activity, that is before the problem or opportunity is even defined. Learners are often guilty of this as well. The point is, the learner must be open to revisiting user requirements or design specifications if the situation indicates it. We prefer the term *activity* to *phase* to discourage the thinking that planning and design are compartmentalized sequential efforts.

5.2. Design

We adopt a broad view of design in our teaching. This view includes technical and social considerations. We view design as integrative in nature. The effective designer is one who can reconcile the technical and the social context within which technology is used to meet the client's need. . Design reflects the designer's *intent* as informed by the social context of use. To the extent that design work is *in the open* – that is, practiced within a social context – it has to be informed by such a balance of concerns to be effective.

The *product* of design is a set of technical specifications. The design document specifies the technical solution and typically includes product, price and vendor information. The design product has a technical core to it, but the process of design is essentially a social process. Designers work with users and others in the client organization through a social process of interpersonal interaction. ICTs are shaped by social forces, and the design process is the arena for stakeholders to press their interests to shape the solution to their preference. Done well, the design process offers users a *way in* to the design and allows them to see the emergent design as relevant to their needs. Asking orienting questions centered on the actual use of the imagined system may allow the apprentice designer to see a *way in* to the design as well. We have found prototypes – paper representations and working system models – to be extremely useful interpretive tools. Prototypes offer users and designers a *way in* to the design. As such, they are also *empowering* tools.

5.3. Learning Through Prototyping

When a technology is made concrete, as in a prototype, its social dimension is highlighted. A prototype may be a paper representation of the imagined system or an actual working model of it. It emphasizes the construction and assembly of artifacts from technological components. It can help ground the imagined abstraction in *a local habitation and a name* – that is, in social processes and practices the user is familiar with. A paper representation – a diagram of the imagined system – can aid figurative thinking in the user. A system prototype can provide a three-dimensional approximation of the imagined system and permit the user to "test drive" it under actual work conditions. It can be a powerful design aid but may not always be feasible to build. For projects that continue beyond a semester, we recommend that the student team build a system prototype as a step before the design is finalized. We support the team with technology resources for building the prototype through the Community and Information Technology Institute (CITI); CITI is described in Chapter 5. For the standard one semester-long project, we require teams to develop a paper representation – this is usually a diagrammatic, functional representation of the imagined system.

When a technology is made concrete in a prototype, it becomes an artifact located in a social space and derives its meaning(s) from the contexts it may be used in. A prototype externalizes the imagined system and facilitates critique and modification by users and other stakeholders. This leads to refinement of the prototype and further critique of it in iterative fashion until a good fit is achieved between user needs and system features. The epistemological process occasioned by the prototype parallels *constructionism* – the prototype promotes learning by both designer and user by externalizing and concretizing abstractions. A prototype helps bring design activity into the open. It serves as a resource for participation and reflection.

Prototyping work helps integrate generalized knowledge with situated knowledge in a powerful way. The learner brings generalized (or *vertical*) knowledge (Stiglitz, 2000) to the situation: knowledge of planning methods and models, knowledge of technology. But she has to learn about the specific situation – the people, the work practices and the culture that characterize that particular environment at that particular time – before she can respond meaningfully to the problem or opportunity she is faced with. This situated (or *horizontal*) knowledge must be acquired *in situ* by the learner working with people at the client site. Such knowledge may have the following qualities: it is emergent, locally embedded, contingent (on local interpretations), and vague (because, to some degree, it may be tacitly held; that is, people at the client site may not be able to articulate what they know). The learner has to work hard to get at this knowledge.

Prototypes can also ground the learner in a social web of relations, dependencies and contracts. She has to work with clients, users, fellow learners, and with vendors and technology service providers (depending on the nature of the prototype) to develop the prototype, in the process giving rise to (and becoming subject to, at the same time) a social web based on cooperation and collective work. She learns by doing and by being a part of the work of others in that social context.

A recent prototyping project illustrates these benefits. The supervisor of a Medicaid program in the county caught a demonstration of Internet videoconferencing over digital subscriber line (DSL) technology put on by our group and was interested in trying it out with his program. We took it on as a project. The prototype linked the Medicaid offices and a city hospital for video interviewing of applicants for Medicaid benefits. The hospital was a major Medicaid applicant intake point. From the outset, the prototype was viewed very differently by the participating organizations. The supervisor, who ran this particular Medicaid program and was responsible for expediting benefit certification decisions, saw video interviewing as a boon and gave the project high visibility within the county. The hospital, which participated in the trial at the supervisor's suggestion, was more guarded and sanctioned the project as a low-profile effort, allocating minimal resources to it. The differences were most telling in the physical space allocated for the video interview. The county dedicated a room to it; the hospital freed up some shared space in a trafficked public area behind a noisy ATM machine. The location was not conducive to conducting a confidential interview for Medicaid benefits certification, to say the least. The supervisor encouraged his staff to participate in the trial and many of them did so enthusiastically. A part of one busy staff member's time was allocated to the effort by the hospital. She had other responsibilities and viewed her participation as an added burden.

The student design team had analyzed the Medicaid benefits certification process prior to the trial and had a good grasp of it. But despite this, they were unprepared for the way video interviewing altered work at the sites. The hospital's fiscal officer complained that his staff person had to do more than before. Previously, the interview took place at the county offices. With video, the interview now occurred at the hospital. The staff person had to photocopy the applicant's financial documents (a dossier could be up to nine inches thick) and sit with the applicant through the interview to help with the technology. These added two hours of extra work on average per applicant to the staff person's schedule.

With video, the county did less than before. The fiscal officer argued that, as the entity solely responsible by law for certifying applicants, the county should be doing more, nor less. Use of video had shifted the power-resources equation to the hospital's detriment. The added burden from video to the hospital could only be justified if the hospital could certify applicants independent of the county. Until that happened, the fiscal officer was skeptical about the innovation's benefits for him. There were many unexpected, positive modifications to work processes and work relations within and between the two sites, but the power-resources imbalance became the sticking point for the hospital for political and economic reasons.

For the user, a prototype can prompt a critical relook at work. The supervisor believed video helped bring his staff and the hospital's staff closer together in a community of practice* dedicated to mutual learning for improved practice. Video, by bringing the hospital's staff directly into the interview and collaborative work with the county's staff, underscored the importance of mutual learning and provided a solution as well. For the apprentice designer, a prototype serves as a lightning rod and searchlight: it provokes user reactions and illuminates the social context of use. It can facilitate *talk-back* (Schon, 1983) from the situation to refine design. Based on evaluation of the trial, the student designers had to rethink system features to address the fiscal officer's concerns.

What happens when prototypes are not used or are used ineffectually in design work? The Urban-net design process was complicated by the poor use of prototypes. The advanced nature of the ICTs was an impediment to broad user participation. Two questions came up repeatedly during the design process: *How will this work?* And *What can it do for me?* Prototypes like the video interviewing system would have transformed the process by answering both questions but were not used by the professional designers from the telephone company who led the process.

The result was that the social shaping of the community network – which started out with egalitarian aims – was highly lopsided. Only those that had the necessary expertise could take part meaningfully in the process. Those that did not could find no way into the imagined system. They had no metaphor, no prototype, to help them find a way into it. The professional designers viewed design as a technical, instrumental activity. They saw the community network as an abstraction, as infrastructure, a generic substrate that could support a variety of uses. Without perhaps intending to, they decontextualized the network. The typical user struggled to contextualize it by imagining familiar uses of it. They viewed the network not as infrastructure but as a set of uses. Not surprisingly, they felt the designs proposed by the professional design staff were inspired by a *cookie-cutter* – generic and context-insensitive. The outcome of this disconnect was disastrous for the typical user (and for the egalitarian ideals that framed the design effort): they failed to see the network as *personally relevant* to their vested interests and concerns and stopped participating in the design.

Design is a situated activity; it occurs within a particular social context. The process is complicated because the terrain can become contested. There may be multiple clients or stakeholders, and they may have divergent views on the design's relevance for them. Satisfying micro-social relevance for one set of stakeholders may come at the expense of what we have called macro-level relevance. The Urban-net design process underlined this dilemma. Design involves choices. It is a political activity. *Relevant for whom?* (i.e. for which user groups) becomes a central question confronting the designer in contested situations.

To summarize, we emphasize the following design truths in our teaching:

Design as interpretation: Design is situated action. It illuminates the link between knowledge and action, between stored knowledge and the contingencies that inform it when it is mobilized and applied in actual situations. "Action has an emergent quality.... Knowledge as organized for a particular task can never be sufficiently detailed, sufficiently precise, to anticipate exactly the conditions or results of actions. Action is never totally controlled by the actor but influenced by the vagaries of the physical and social world" (Cited in Chaiklin & Lave, 1993). As the video interviewing example illustrates, the designers came to understand the design task in the process of working through it. Acting and knowing are interrelated. Donald Schon's (Schon, 1983) term *reflection-in-action* says it well.

We urge our students to develop prototypes – paper representations, working models – whenever possible to aid design communication and reflection. Used well, prototypes can help interpenetrate the designer's *normative* world (normative in that it stems from their understanding of design *constraints*) and the situated world of users, allowing the one to inform the other in fruitful ways. Learners should understand prototypes as vital interpretive aids for themselves as well as for users. Prototypes are best used to loosen and open up design, not close it prematurely. The instructor must be vigilant that design closure does not occur too soon. The prototype should be viewed not so much as a destination as a point of departure for inquiry.

A prototype in play during design has two conflicting roles: to facilitate critical inquiry by the user and the designer into system features and affordances, and to reduce interpretive flexibility. That is, it is intended simultaneously to stimulate design questions and narrow design options. The tension between the two goals has to be managed if the designer wishes to avoid premature closure. In our experience, an effective way to manage this tension is by asking what we term the *critical* question: *How will it work under organizational conditions?* Such a question (or variations of it) links the unfamiliar (imagined system) with the familiar (organizational work processes) and sparks dialogue on system features that are worth saving and those that are not. The system has gained definition but is not yet closed – precisely what a prototype is intended to do. We illustrate the use of critical questioning below in the context of a system prototype developed by our students for a faith-based social action coalition. In this case, the system prototype was developed but not installed at the user site owing to resource constraints. The critical question is indeed crucial in such cases, and where only paper representations are feasible. Where the system prototype is installed at the user site, as in the case of the Medicaid application discussed earlier, answering the critical question should be a main focus of the prototype evaluation effort.

Design as improvisation: As part of the interpretive process, learners generate and test hypotheses about the design task at hand: user needs, technology and design options, the social context of development and use. These hypotheses (or prototypes or conjectures) may be more or less formal or explicit, but learning about the world entails such an *epistemic* process (Kruglanski, 1989), wherein hypotheses are tested until the inquirer is ready to act on the knowledge obtained through the process. We see situated learning as *active, adaptive* inquiry, where the learner continually tests her understanding of the use context and adapts her inquiry (and the design) as needed. She is assumed to be a discoverer. She is assumed not to have perfect information on the design problem or opportunity, nor is she assumed to have perfect rationality.

Our view of design resists both technological and social determinism. It is holistic and socio-technical in its emphasis. Design is not wholly technologically driven, nor can it be informed only by social considerations. All technologies come with inherent material constraints but they also offer design choices within these constraints. There are certain technological requirements that have to be respected by the designer. There are only so many ways that a midrange computer can be integrated into a LAN, and only so many tenable ways that a client/server transaction can be provided for. These technological "ground rules" constrain the solution design space. Within this space, however, there usually is a broad range of candidate solutions that the designer must consider in light of the organization's needs, resources and constraints, its culture, its climate of power. It is in integrating and synthesizing a customized, situated response to the client's need from the options available that we call *improvising*.

Design as relevance engineering: ICTs are a configurable technology (Kling, Crawford, Rosenbaum, Sawyer, and Weisband, 2000). That is, they represent generic capabilities that are customized by the designer to match a specific set of requirements. Configurations are tailored to a particular space and time, and to a group of users. In customizing a configuration, the designer fashions a particular collection of capabilities from those available to meet requirements. The process may be viewed as *relevance engineering*. As the designer progressively particularizes a configuration, it is seen as increasingly more relevant to her needs by the user. Relevance engineering takes skill and empathy and deliberate effort to pull off.

A configurable technology can be shaped in different ways: different configurations are possible. The personal relevance of a particular configuration is judged by the user. It is the designer's responsibility to *facilitate* its shaping by target user groups through the design process. The designer has to ensure that users can find a way in to the design and participation in the process. One way to do this is by asking the critical question: How will the solution work *for the client*? The question looks at technology in its social context of use; it is socio-technical in intent. The designer has to be able to answer the question for herself as well as help the user work through the answer. The Urban-net design effort failed as an open, inclusive activity because it effectively ignored the question.

Design as relevance engineering must be concerned with the content as well as the form of relevance. The *content* of relevance refers to the capabilities of the technology solution that is being designed; the *form* of relevance refers to how the user may invoke – use – these system capabilities. The form is critical; indeed, capabilities are useless if the user cannot easily invoke them. The design must present the user with easy to understand points of entry into the system – these could consist of icons and commands, these could also be orienting social cues like stories and metaphors. A student team helped a client use a scanner by likening it to a copying machine: *Just slide the sheet in, just like you would with the Xerox machine.* We emphasize the interconnectedness of the two – the content and form of relevance. Ensuring that the designed artifact is relevant in the *formal* sense may mean training the user, developing manuals to guide the user, and being available to help trouble-shoot problems when they arise. In the case of the Medicaid video interviewing prototype, the student teams provided extended support to users, including training, manual development and trouble-shooting assistance in the initial months after installation. Thinking about the extended support infrastructure as comprising human and automated help amenities gets the learner thinking about design in a new and more responsible way. Designing an artifact does not end with the artifact; rather, it begins there and fans outward from there to enclose a whole support environment (Margolin, 1995).

A recent class project illustrated the value of this approach powerfully to our students. The student team researched an Internet fax solution for a faith-based social action coalition. The coalition wanted to reach its constituents quickly and cheaply, and fax communication over the Internet was a cost-effective option. The system would send the message out as an email to those constituents who had an Internet connection and as fax to those that did not.

Mid-way through the semester, the team made an initial presentation to the client on Internet faxing. The coalition was technology-poor, and the team wanted to test their level of comfort with the solution. The students started the presentation with a generic technical overview of Internet faxing. This was a mistake; attendees were not interested. Their eyes glazed over. Then one of them asked the students to show how Internet faxing would work for them: "*Rev. _____ has to get the word out. How would he use this?*" The Internet fax software had to set up first with the list of email addresses and fax numbers. The fax server (a personal computer that handled all incoming and outgoing messages) and the *attached* printer would have to be maintained and upgraded as needed to ensure they worked well; this called for at-hand technical support. It also called for an always-on Internet connection. If the coalition could not afford an always-on connection, policies would have to be developed for dialing in to the Internet at certain times of the day and night. How would such an arrangement affect the coalition's need to get the word out on breaking events in a timely manner? Some constituents had the opposite need: Would they be able to get a weekly digest of the information if they wished? In explaining how it worked, the students gained a grounded and localized appreciation of the system. In answering users' questions, they were forced to think of the system less as generic technology and more as a solution to a specific problem, and less in technical terms and more as a socio-technical ensemble consisting of technology and an infrastructure to support it. By semester's end, what had been *dry* to the client and the students had become *wet* (personally relevant) to both through *the* design process. The user's questions showed both students and the client a *way in* to the design and allowed them to think productively about the artifact and its use environment. The object became socialized both for the client and the team, meaningful within a social context.

5.4. Tying Together Planning And Design

To summarize, planning involves problem setting, and design involves specifying the solution. The design that is proposed by learners should logically flow from the problem as defined.

Without adequate planning, the consultant only has indeterminate criteria for evaluating the goodness of fit of design recommendations. By what criteria is one design superior to another? Further, when the planning effort is truncated, the role of the context of use in shaping the design is curtailed, and the resulting product is usually deficient. Compelling as the logical connection between planning and design may seem, learners often are impatient to start on the design. Design tends to be a more concrete in that it involves technology and technical considerations. It can be a better- defined activity relative to planning, and as such more attractive to learners. We actively discourage learners from cutting short the planning effort.

We use a relatively simple strategy to get learners to link design outcomes to the criteria and values defined through planning. The field project assignment requires consultant teams to research and document at least two comparable candidate designs and recommend one to the client for adoption. We require both options to be documented in the team's final report, followed by the recommendation and its justification: Why was one option preferred over the other? This encourages learners to reflect on their design choices: How is one configuration superior to another? By what criteria might the choice(s) be justified? It gets them to think of alternative configurations through the lens of the client's requirements. The team must establish a reasoned correspondence between the design product and the planning product. The importance of such a linking for sound practice is emphasized throughout the semester.

Justification of the recommended design is critical for another reason: it permits an independent reader (the client, the instructor, learners in future semesters) to follow the reasoning behind the choice and judge its robustness. The ability to reason about design choices is a hallmark of professional work, as the theorist Richard Buchanan (1995, p. 83) has argued:

> Making involves two components. The first is the actual work of fabrication...the second is the ability to explain and demonstrate the results of fabrication based on reasons or principles. The ability to explain is an integral part of making: it enables the maker to judge the progress of work at each stage and, equally important, persuade

colleagues, clients, and consumers that a particular product is effective for a given situation. Makers who only possess the skills of work simply practice a trade at the direction of others. Those who also understand and can explain the basis of their work are "architectons"— master craftsman, master builders, architects, engineers, and in general, those who are capable of directing their own work and the work of others.

6. AN EXTENDED MODEL OF ACTIVE LEARNING

Over the years, we have developed and refined a model of active learning using the project assignment as the stimulus. Our model builds on and extends the work of the learning theories outlined earlier. Our intent has been and continues to be utilitarian: to outline a framework for acting and learning in the field. We make no claims about the model's completeness. It is a work in progress; it continues to evolve. What we present here is an extended reflection on using the model in our teaching at the collegiate level. The model is based on four basic principles, and draws on research and practice in organizational work, active learning, motivation, and community service learning. The statement of each principle is followed by a description of steps we have taken (and the challenges we have faced) in operationalizing it in our own teaching practice.

6.1. Principle # 1. Client-centered work in natural settings

Active learning that requires the learner to provide a deliverable to an identifiable client (or customer) has significant motivational benefits for the learner. The client plays an important role in professional education. Indeed, the idea of professionalism itself is often defined with reference to the client: "since the essence of professionalism is the delivery of a service in response to a client need, it becomes critical, if the professional is to retain his sense of professional identity, to identify clearly on whose behalf services are being rendered" (Schein & Kommers 1972, p.22). Active learning with a client in clear view is more effective than when this is not the case.

In *Professional education: Some new direction* (1972), Schein and Kommers analyze the changing role of the client in the professions and notes the following:

-   The term "client" increasingly refers to an organization and not an individual.
-   There may be more than one client for professional services in an organization.
-   Schein and Kommers differentiate between immediate or contact, intermediate and ultimate clients (the users). The ultimate client's needs may conflict with that of the immediate or intermediate client.
-   Practitioners have to learn how to involve the ultimate client in decisions.
-   Practitioners have to learn how to "reconcile or integrate the needs of the individual with those of the community or society as a whole".

Learners in natural environments quickly realize how important knowing the client is. In the example of the local government agency earlier, the student team had to acknowledge multiple clients. The administrative officer was the contact or immediate client, his staff (users of the database) were the intermediate client, and users of the information in the database (the district attorney, members of the public) were the ultimate clients. The team worked directly with the contact and intermediate clients; the contact client communicated the ultimate clients' needs to the team. But behind the contact client were the techies who maintained the mainframe: this group was powerful and influential but refused to play any substantive role in the project (Schein and Kommers, 1972). The student team's project activities were circumscribed and manipulated by the techies. The contact client understood the problem but was helpless, and could get only one half of his project goals (implementing a local area network in his office) accomplished.

The contact client (the administrative officer) represented the ultimate clients and their needs. The team did an extensive planning analysis on-site, collecting data through interviews, surveys and analysis of archival documentation (e.g., database printouts and reports). The project provided students an excellent, first-hand experience with several of Schein and Kommer's injunctions: the client was an organization, there were multiple clients some of whom were unacknowledged (the techies), and there was an unproductive and unresolved tension between the acknowledged and unacknowledged clients. The team had to manage relations with both sets of clients. In the case of the administrative officer and the user group, the team had to manage expectations as the project scope shrank in the face of non-cooperation from the techies. Vis-à-vis the techies, the team had to come across as flexible yet professional. A focus on the customer quickly sensitizes learners to the importance of managing client relations, a skill that professional programs do not adequately cover.

Schein and Kommers' last point is akin to our *macro-social relevance*, outlined earlier in the chapter. The director of a branch public library wanted a wireless network installed to connect her library, which was in a poor area of the city, and a neighboring building that housed a church. The network would permit outside access to the library's technological resources – information CD-ROMs, the online public access catalog, Internet, the PCs in the Computer Lab for skills learning. The director knew that the county library system intended to use the Urban-net – the advanced technology community network alluded to earlier – to link all branch libraries to other public institutions in the community. Nonetheless, she wanted to explore wireless to link to the church for a number of reasons: the Urban-net was taking too long, and while she supported the idea of the Urban-net she wished to be financially independent of the county library bureaucracy with respect to technology decisions; she wished to be entrepreneurial and seek external funding to fund the wireless network. She was looking to the team for the design and financial information she would need to talk to funding sources.

In their final report, the team designed a wireless network for the client. But they also listed the benefits to the library of being linked to the Urban-net. The Urban-net would significantly amplify its reach: linking to other community institutions (such as K-12 schools and local churches) would give the library access to an expanded set of patrons and enriched multi-media information resources. With wireless, the library would have to bear the capital and recurring costs, both of which were significant. Linking to the Urban-net would be cheaper due to the economics of bulk buying: capital and recurring costs would be shared by subscribers and negotiated collectively by them as a buying group. Prior to this project, no one on the team had had to think about wireless technology for a real-world user against viable alternative technologies. In the process, they learned to view the client's need in relation to the larger community, duly noting the opportunities that would open up for innovative service delivery to new populations over the Urban-net. In short, the library could do more at lower cost with the Urban-net than it could with the wireless network. The client has since given up on wireless and expects to be on the Urban-net with the rest of the county library system.

Client-centered work in natural settings can be challenging. In cases with multiple clients, learners receive conflicting directives reflective of conflicting priorities. There is no formula to deal with such issues. Some teams decide to work around conflict. One recent team, for example, aligned its work with the priorities of the technical group (the contact client) at the client site and left it up to the technical head to sort things out with a powerful functional area manager, who wanted the team to focus on *his* priorities. Other teams work through conflict: the team working on the local government agency project tried unsuccessfully to include the techies in the project and even tried to bring them to the table along with other stakeholders. Typically, the politics are not intractable and the differences of opinion, not irreconcilable. Nonetheless, dealing with such issues is invaluable for professional education: students learn to think carefully about who the players are and who they should satisfy first. The choices they make affect project outcomes.

A second challenge stems from a fairly common dilemma: should the team confirm a choice that the client has already made or is seriously considering, or recommend what they believe is the better alternative? We advice students to recommend what their research indicates is the optimal solution. However, we encourage them to research the client's preferred option before accepting or rejecting it. The technical head at a client site had picked a networking design before signing on for a project. He was looking for the team to endorse his choice. However, the team's research showed that going with his option would entail replacing the 50 or so PCs at the site with newer machines – an expensive proposition. The team used their analysis to successfully argue against the technical head's solution. In such situations, students are doing much more than weigh the pros and cons of technological alternatives; they are confronting basic issues of professional identity, conduct and integrity.

Managing client relations includes managing expectations. Clients want it all in one shot. Planning, design and implementation: many clients want it all done in one semester. By the end of it they have learned that this is not feasible or even desirable: the extent of organizational disruption would be too high for comfort. Many clients have remarked that the most important thing they learned from the project is that technology adoption can be piecemeal and gradual. But before this point is reached, teams may spend a good chunk of planning time negotiating problem boundaries with the client. The instructor has to work with the client to manage expectations about the relationship. By signing on as a client, the organization agrees to support student learning. Implicit in this is the understanding that the reports are the work of apprentices, not full-fledged professionals. Further, although the consulting service is provided free of charge, the client has to be willing to sustain non-monetary costs, primarily staff time. The client has to understand that they have responsibilities too. They have to agree to support the project, designate a contact person on site, and visit the class for their initial presentation and again at the end of the semester, for the presentation of the final report by the student teams.

6.2. Principle # 2. apprenticeship learning through participation

Learning comes from doing and from the social aspects of participation in activities that are personally meaningful to the learner. That is, attaining competence in a subject area involves active learning in natural settings with and through other similarly engaged learners.

The apprentice learner starts out as a legitimate peripheral participant (Lave, 1993). She learns by doing peripheral things at first, but the work she participates in along with other learners under a master practitioner is real: in other words, the context is actual work practice. As she becomes progressively more proficient, she moves toward full participation in the activity. Eventually, she becomes a master practitioner in her own right. This view of learning emphasizes the following ideas. The learner is an apprentice; she learns by doing in the actual context of work – the natural work setting. She learns by actively taking part in a community of practice (Lave and Wenger, 1991) – which includes other apprentices like herself and master practitioners. Participation in this social milieu develops her skills as well as her identity (Lave, 1993) as a competent professional. Lastly, learning through participation in actual practice as a member of a cohort highlights opportunities for peer learning and skill development.

Students enrolled in our classes come from diverse backgrounds. Some are trained in library and information science, business, humanities, and communication, while others have a background in engineering and computer science. Undergraduates as well as graduate students enroll in the class (this has changed now). Team composition, usually done by the instructor, attempts to balance skills and skill levels in the team, so that technically-adept students get to work with students with other skills. This is a way to spread technical skills around, as well as to simulate cross-functional teams in actual organizations. This approach to team composition has worked well. In our experience, students with technical skills tend to lead the design effort, while playing a support role in the planning. Students with a background in the humanities feel more comfortable leading the planning effort, which entails interpersonal communication and listening skills, note-taking and documentation, team work coordination and qualitative inquiry skills (e.g., interviewing). This division of labor happens naturally, and despite our attempts to direct students to acquire skills in areas of deficiency. In terms of the idea of legitimate peripheral participation, non-technical team members can be seen as peripheral participants in design, while technical members are peripheral participants in planning. Fostering peer learning across member competencies can be a challenge; instructors cannot assume this would occur naturally. Knowledge and information handoffs between peripheral and "central" members may not be, and usually is not, seamless or automatic.

Probably the biggest challenge for the instructor is this: how to get the peripheral participant to see *the big picture*? Students heavily involved in the planning may not have the background to understand, or may be unwilling to make the effort to understand, the technical design details of a solution, and vice versa. In highly-motivating task situations, members usually are enthusiastic and proactive about learning from peers to fill in the gaps in their own training and background, but such an outcome cannot be assumed. It needs to be guided and channelized by the instructor.

Peer learning across member competencies is a necessity in project teams with differential skills and skill levels. The model of legitimate peripheral participation offers a provocative perspective on peer learning in such project teams without specifying how such learning occurs in practical terms. Recall that the assignment (the field project assignment, described earlier) requires that the student team justify their choice from the two comparable candidate solutions considered under the project. Justifying the choice is critical. It forces the team to consider their recommendation carefully and critically. It permits an independent reader to assess the suitability of the recommended solution (versus the rejected candidate) and the logic underlying the conclusion. Most importantly, it forces the team to revisit the client's needs, resources and constraints in assessing the goodness of fit of the recommended solution. The planning effort, when done well, yields *the* criteria for such an assessment – these criteria might be technical and non-technical, and are of fundamental importance and relevance in a client-driven learning exercise. The written justification of the team's choice is prominently emphasized in the assignment and orally in class several times during the semester. We believe that this piece – the justification of the choice – is a powerful way of bringing to bear on design the concerns of planning, and to encourage – force – the *center* and the *periphery* to educate each other through the project.

The peripheral participant has to have a clear sense of how her work relates to the rest of the project. In complex projects, there is the danger that the peripheral participant would do her bit and then disengage from the rest of the project, perhaps because she lacks the substantive skills to see the linkages (there may be other reasons as well, but lack of requisite skills is a particular problem in heterogeneous teams). The *periphery-center* information handoff challenge has to be consciously managed for learner self-development and peer learning to occur. A peripheral participant needs to understand how her contribution fits into the whole. Understanding the part-whole link can have positive motivational implications for the learner. We primarily use class time to address process (*how-to*) and substantive (knowledge) aspects of this hand-off problem between individual work and teamwork. Automated tools can be useful as well. However, since student teams tend to work in less structured environments relative to organizational work teams, we have found the class listserv to be of limited value in this role; as a lean medium, it is not rich enough to adequately engage the many open-ended issues that may come up.

A community of peers engaged in active learning in the field helps *decenter* learning, which refers to shifting the source of learning from the instructor to the totality of resources available to the learner in that environment. The instructor's pedagogical role shifts from being a source of wisdom to a knowledgeable guide who helps identify, qualify and structure knowledge resources in the decentered learning environment. On our teams, such resources include other team members, as well as the consultants (some on-campus, most off), vendors and service providers, and former students that the team may consult via the Internet, phone, or meet face to face, formally or informally, during the course of the project. For example, a team needing help on a critical issue relating to data sharing between an AS-400 (a type of midrange computer) and a LAN contacted a former student who was then on the IS staff of a major firm in the area and obtained detailed information on a similar solution he had successfully implemented in his firm. Project work allows learners to tap into a supportive web in the local community and beyond, and helps link learning and socialization in professional practice. For the majority of our students, the project provides their first opportunity to do hands-on consulting work; interacting with practitioners through the project contributes to their emergent self-image as "professionals", and this self-image, and the competencies it subsumes, is an important reason why many find the experience "fun" and "rewarding".

The client (or representative) herself may start out as a peripheral participant on the project team. The interested technician or MIS staffer at the client site (very rarely has it been a non-technical staffer) may start out as project contact, begins to learn by participating in the work of the team, and acquires enough knowledge at semester end to want to play a bigger role on the project the following semester. Participation by the client in the work of the team is valuable for a number of reasons. First, participation allows the client to be a better client. To look at the project from the participant's viewpoint is to better appreciate the challenges faced by the team in their work. Second, participation allows the client to improve their understanding of technology and can, over time, contribute to an improved ability to make informed decisions about technology. Promoting self-sufficiency among non-profits and public sector institutions in technology know-how is an important objective of our outreach effort; the client's peripheral participation is a start. Third, participation shifts the client from a *reactive user* to an active force in the developmental context. An active client can represent the user in a very different light to the team, and can help change the way they think about technology. For example, the MIS head in a community agency sensitized the team to the need for creative new assistive applications to empower his office staff, all of whom were disabled. While this was outside the project's scope and was therefore not pursued that semester, he prompted the team to think of the infrastructure they were designing as eventually supporting a far broader range of uses than the typical user may have outlined.

6.3. Principle # 3. The social context of professional action

The practice of active learning in the service of the community acquires its special resonance from linking learning to the broader life of the community. As we noted earlier, for most of our students, the project provides their first real introduction to the local community – not just to the client organization but to the larger socioeconomic concerns that often form the backdrop for that organization's work and the reason for its existence. Our community has one of the highest child mortality rates nationally, and a high adolescent pregnancy rate. These statistics seldom intrude into campus life. Yet they are central to the work of community-based organizations operating in the human services area, and project work in these locations exposes students to a dimension of community life they rarely suspect exists.

This macro-social dimension may not directly impact their design. Recall the earlier distinction between the micro-social and the macro-social. Micro-social sensitivity is called for when the designer designs an artifact – a computer interface or physical access to a building – taking into account the needs of disabled users. Macro-level sensitivity emphasizes the larger issues – such as inequity in access to computers and networked resources that has been labeled the Digital Divide. Macro-level awareness may not instrumentally inform the design of particular artifacts, but it can provide a perspective on *logically prior* concerns – such as access, raising questions such as: Why is it that whole sections of a community are out of the loop in terms of access to computing? How can technology advance the work of relief agencies? Such questions lie in the *moral* domain. Such questions are fundamental to the function of design in contemporary society, we believe, and provide a values-based perspective on the design enterprise.

A human service institution representing the poorer sections of the Hispanic community had many technology needs: internal networking, Internet connectivity, high bandwidth connectivity to county offices for video-conferencing to help streamline administration of the many public assistance programs it handled. The design recommended by the team was cost-effective; the report took pains to argue the need for a cost-effective solution given the agency's resources and constraints; the design was unremarkable from the viewpoint of micro-level sensitivity. However, the team got a powerful sense of the broad social goals to which their design was a contributor (the proposed design is being implemented), and this helped highlight the importance of their work for the client and the community at large. Also highlighted was the *moral* imperative of such work, which we emphasize in class at the beginning of each semester. The institution would not have considered the more advanced applications (such as video-conferencing) without the team's help, simply because it lacked technological know-how. But now the institution, and its clientele, many of whom are indeed the digital have-nots referenced under the Digital Divide, will have access to advanced technology. Micro-level sensitivity is *topical* and local; macro-level sensitivity, on the other-hand, needs to be *pervasive* and fundamental to design.

A community institution serving the needs of the hearing-impaired was hard-pressed to meet the demand for signing (sign language) services. Its signing experts spent a lot of time commuting to where their services were needed, time that could have been better spent signing. The institution's executive director saw a live demonstration of video-conferencing over DSL over the Internet; the demo was put on by a student team from one of our classes. He immediately saw video as a solution to his problem. His agency is being helped to get on board the community-wide video-conferencing network our student teams are currently implementing. It is important that micro-level concerns be kept in view. For example, the video output had to match the pace of the signer; this is currently not easy to do with off-the-shelf systems. Without such customization, the solution may not be very usable, raising questions of access and use at the *micro-level*. These are very important questions. However, such questions come after the logically prior concern: that is, advanced technology solutions typically are out of reach for such applications because of structural lacks – such as lack of technical and social support infrastructure in human service institutions. Such lacks are correctible (e.g., through outreach), but because they exist, whole sections in a community cannot access technology and its benefits. Realizing this is to realize the moral imperative of professional action, and that of civic engagement and participation in the context of service learning – a point we emphasize in our classes.

Through the project experience, students get a good feel for the constraints under which non-profit and public sector institutions often function. Constraints define the problem or problems that design work attempts to solve: there are no problems without constraints. Constraints can be of different kinds: physical (e.g., site location), financial, technology-related. Constraints can be hidden and may only surface during the design process. The computing culture – the degree of receptivity to the innovation – may be one such. Although one can get a sense of this during planning, its true extent often only becomes apparent during design, when the solution is concretized and specified. The LAN design project at the county department described earlier is an excellent case in point. The MIS department's distrust of LAN technology was quite well known in the user organization, but it hardened and deepened during the course of the project and expressed itself in open hostility towards the team by the end of it. Public institutions and community-based organizations, especially the latter, abound in constraints. Constraints force the learner to be creative and resourceful. Combining service learning and client-centered work yokes together a service orientation with critical thinking, because the team ultimately is accountable to the client.

6.4. *Principle # 4.* Project task design

The project task has to be highly motivating to the learner. Task motivation is but one determinant of task performance (the prevailing reward system, for example, is a known motivator of performance in teamwork), but it is one that can be designed rather easily into the stimulus by the instructor. Task design influences learner behavior: the extent to and depth at which knowledge is processed, the level of performance, and the willingness to go the extra mile for the client may all be influenced through task design.

We have found Hackman and Oldham's (1982) task motivational principles useful in our design of the stimulus. A task high in these characteristics is known to promote motivation:

- It is a whole and meaningful piece of work, with a visible outcome.
- It requires members to use a variety of relatively high-level skills.
- The outcome of the team's work has significant consequences for the client and others.
- It provides learners with substantial autonomy for deciding about how they do the work; the team is responsible for the work and the outcomes.
- Work on the task generates regular feedback on the team's performance.

The task is fairly tightly defined and delimited at the outset to increase the chance that the team will be able to complete it satisfactorily in a semester. We as instructors work with the client in advance to define the tasks – or project *topics* – for the teams. Wireless connectivity between the library and the church: this is an example of a topic definition. It is expected that the team would further refine the topic through interaction with the client as the project picks up speed. Task foci, priorities, boundaries: these may all be (and usually are) negotiated by the team with the client. Should the Urban-net supersede wireless networks as the focus of the project? Learners in a team may push for task scope redefinition based on feasibility and resource availability within the team: If the client wants a wireless network prototype in place at semester's end, can the team do it? Should they recommend that the prototyping be undertaken the following semester by a different team? Sometimes a team may push to expand the scope of the task for it to be a meaningful piece of work. Defining the task is a challenge: questions of feasibility should be weighed carefully against the integrity of the individual topic. The learners' interests and that of the client have to be reconciled; the task engaged by the team has to be meaningful to the team and the client.

Task definition can be a particular challenge under certain conditions. What if the library had needed help with Internet connectivity in addition to wireless connectivity to the church? Internet connectivity usually qualifies as its own topic. To make an informed choice, a client will need information on Internet Service Providers offering services in the area, types of services provided and their costs, and changes that subscription may entail to the client's on-site technology infrastructure. Should the library connect to the church over the Internet? Defining the task thus collapses the two topics – church connectivity and Internet connectivity – into one, enabling the students to explore potential synergies between connectivity options and targets. But such a redefinition may or may not meet the needs of the client, who may want the topics examined independently.

If the decision is made to go with two independent topics, it would necessitate coordinating the efforts of the teams involved. The client at some point in the future might wish to combine the Internet connectivity option with that of church connectivity if it makes sense to do so. It would be useful to the teams involved to be briefed about each other's work as the project unfolds. We, as instructors, have taken on the burden of coordinating the work of the teams in such cases. Through in-class discussions centered on the assignment and in meetings with students outside class, we update the teams on each other's work and highlight areas of common concern. We suggest that the teams keep each other's work in view when recommending their solution in the final report. By helping transfer information between them, we allow the teams to focus on their topic. Satisfactory completion of the project within the available time (one semester) is important for the team and the client. Inter-team coordination, however, is critical, and the instructor's role as boundary spanner is a key to achieving coherence and synergy overall in the consulting effort.

As noted above, the requirement that the team justify the design recommendation helps integrate the planning and design activities in a team. Prototypes – paper or system – help convey a visual sense of the solution to both client and learner.

Skill variety. The project assignment calls for team effort. Its scope is considerable and the skills required diverse enough for a team-level effort. Recall that the project consists of two parts: planning and design. Planning calls for many skills: interviewing, listening, writing, client relations and project management, and surveying and data analysis skills. People skills are critical in planning, as is tolerance for ambiguity. The planner is a fact collector and explorer, a sensitive inquirer and change agent. Design ability calls for a high proportion of technical skills. The designer fits solutions to what the planner uncovers. But design is as much a social activity as planning. Student teams may work with experts in the community and consult others by phone and over the Internet in assembling their recommendation. They may talk to vendors and service providers, and with alums of the class, about design. When we present the project assignment in class at the start of the semester, we urge students to keep these diverse skill requirements in mind when forming project teams.

Work of significance to the client: Clients value their participation in the project. Many have implemented solutions recommended by student teams; others have used project reports to complete grant proposals for funding. Yet others have used the project politically, as a goad to get their staff to do things. Symbolically and/or substantively, project outcomes usually are significant to the client.

Autonomy: The student team selects the project topic. After the client presents in class (this occurs early in the semester), students pick the topic they want to work on. We believe strongly that students have to be interested in what they do. Unfortunately, this also means there is no guarantee that every one of the client's needs will be met through the class that semester. That is, some topics may not attract any "bids" from teams and may go unsubscribed as a result. Clients understand this. We advise them to market their needs in class, to put a little sales spin on their presentation, to help improve the odds of being picked by a team. A second implication is that more than one team may pick the same project topic. We allow this. But we also make it clear that the teams should file separate final reports. They are welcome to work together but they are also encouraged to explore ideas independently; what they turn in at the end of the semester must be their considered opinion. Occasionally, we have persuaded teams to take on unsubscribed topics, but this is only done when interest in the class is starkly lop-sided.

Student teams enjoy considerable autonomy. They are essentially self-managing task groups. Project tasks are assigned by the team to its members. Monitoring of progress and regulation of member behavior is also the responsibility of the team. The team is free to fire members as a last resort, but in consultation with the instructor. The team is responsible for managing client relations and the timely completion of all project deliverables. This does not mean teams are left to fend for themselves. The class is a supportive, nurturing environment, and class time is set aside to discus project progress and address problems. We work closely with the student teams through the course of the project, offering help with task and interpersonal issues.

Feedback: Student teams get regular feedback from two sources during the project: from the class and from the client. From about the mid-point of the semester onwards, project-related discussions are a part of every class meeting. Discussing a project in class allows students from unrelated projects to offer suggestions and ideas to the project team. The instructor plays coach during these discussions, orienting the team as needed, acting as a sounding board for suggestions from the team and the class, identifying design weaknesses and strengths. Class discussions can get really lively mid-semester, as projects heat up and deadlines loom.

Formative feedback from the client occurs at many points during the project; every meeting offers potential for critique. Formal sign-offs are not required from the client; this would be intimidating to many. Informal sign-offs, however, are encouraged, before the team starts on the next activity. Clients have the opportunity to offer summative feedback to the team when they attend the presentation of the final report at the end of the semester. They are invited by the team(s) to attend the in-class presentation, and they get the first shot at quizzing their team(s) on the project.

It is difficult to conceive of a new generation of systems consultants graduating without an appreciation of the inequities in the distribution of technology, technology use skills and access to networked information. Building a socially-aware service learning program into a college curriculum can serve two ends: it is a powerful way to sensitize tomorrow's technical professionals to these inequities, and it is a way to build a locally sustainable way to address the technical skills gap in the Digital Divide. One of the major challenges of technology change is to sustain the momentum after its introduction. User training and technology upgrades are ongoing needs. Technology solutions often fail from lack of knowledge resources to support them. Further, the adopting organization has to find a way to stay open to new ideas, and to develop vendor-independent consultants to ensure that it is not buying into obsolete solutions. Lack of technical know-how can be a barrier to technology adoption even in the corporate sector (Attewell, 1992). This barrier is significant among CBOs. The know-how barrier is particularly problematic in community networking projects like the Urban-net, which was premised on enabling community - wide access to networked resources. University-based learning-in-community initiatives can play a critical leveling role with respect to technical know-how and help democratize access.

Community outreach programs have been in existence for a number of years in academic settings, focused on training community developers to work in underserved areas in the U.S. and developing nations through active involvement in community development initiatives. A similar need exists in the more technically oriented programs of study in higher education, as community development and urban revitalization programs themselves are increasingly tied to information technology.

Service learning experiences in technical consulting offers a powerful means for students to see first-hand the effects of the Digital Divide on people and service institutions and to actively engage in changing the situation. Students see the link between the dry statistics of such deprivation and the work of agencies in their own community that are forced to face them on a daily basis. Locating the service learning experience in the community makes for a qualitatively different experience than a coop stint at a for-profit entity: the difference stems directly from the service component. It is our experience that students relate extremely well to volunteerism and service if they are seen as concrete (i.e. the student can actively participate in it in a meaningful way) and relevant to their area of study; many view the project experience as akin to doing field research on technology transfer and organizational change-agentry. Our students have reported high levels of satisfaction that their work helped a needy client; some have chosen to continue their work for the client under an independent study or internship arrangement, or simply as a volunteer, even after the project's completion. Student evaluations of the project experience have also mentioned: a heightened sense of self-efficacy, confidence that change can be initiated in small steps, better appreciation of the needs of the needy, satisfaction with change-agent role (that they helped "make a difference"), improved knowledge of the local community, and respect for non-profits' work.

As instructional designers, we have modified our active learning approach based on what our students and clients have told us. We started out with a notion of what active learning should encompass, and refined it after several years of experimentation in the field. Our ideas are still evolving; we make no claims about the completeness or generalizability of the model presented above. This works for us, for now, but it is also a work in progress.

CHAPTER 3

LOCATING LEARNING

1. INTRODUCTION

Active learning can occur anywhere. Providing opportunities to the learner to actively engage in the experience of comprehending, reflecting and doing – acting out the learning – can be done in a laboratory setting, in a classroom using a case study as stimulus, or out in the "field" – under actual living and working conditions. The instructor may not have a choice always in terms of the location. Some types of questions and areas of learning call for a laboratory and are best engaged there. Evaluating different ICT design options on user attitudes may be an example; evaluations of this type would be far easier to attempt in a controlled setting. A case study is very well suited to stimulate thinking and learning on the effects of automation on worker displacement in industries with varying degrees of labor organization. Here again, the criterion of feasibility would recommend the case study method versus study in the field. A case study would be able to cover more ground, by simulating conditions in a greater variety of industries more efficiently and perhaps even more effectively than would be possible by other means. Such methods have significant strengths even if the instructor could avail of field-based instructional methods. We are not arguing for the superiority of learning-in-community over these others. However, for our purposes, we have found the field – the non-profit sector in the immediate geographical community – to be invaluable as an enabler of the kind of learning we wish to foster

As we noted in the previous chapter, our approach to active learning is to locate it in the proximate community. Engaging real problems in real organizational settings can provide important benefits to the learner. We discussed the four levers of our approach: client-centered work, learning through social participation, task motivation, and the social side of professional action. We focus on the last in this chapter – in particular, we discuss the historical opportunity for greater professional involvement in the proximate community and how our teaching has responded to it. The learning-in-community opportunity we provide through our classes has helped our students appreciate, albeit in a limited sense, the social benefits that professionals can bring to some of the neediest constituents in the locality they live in. Clearly, transformation – in terms of change in the learner's values and in the broader social context of their action – is a complex process over time and no class or single course of study, however intensive or elaborate, can hope to accomplish it. Our classes simply provide one opportunity (for many of our students they have tended to be the first) for students to get involved in what we term technological activism – civic engagement locally in a technical consulting capacity.

Underlying our approach to locating learning in the proximate community are the ideas of John Dewey. As a pragmatist, Dewey believed in the civic responsibility of education through humane action. His view of the educational enterprise is centrally relevant to the ideas discussed in the last chapter and to the objective of the present one.

> To learn in a humane way and to humane effect is not just to acquire added skill through refinement of original capacities. To learn to be human is to develop through the give-and-take of communication an effective sense of being an individual distinct member of a community; one who understands and appreciates its beliefs, desires and methods, and who contributes to a further conversion of organic powers into human resources and values (Dewey, 1927, p. 21).

2. A DIFFERENT DIMENSION OF THE DIGITAL DIVIDE

The Digital Divide – the gap between those with access to ICT and those without – has been called "one of America's leading economic and civil rights issues"(U.S. Department of Commerce Report, 1999). The divide is pervasive, and it appears to be growing. However, present characterizations of the divide are mainly concerned with individual and household access to ICT devices – computers, telephone modem and the Internet. Access to ICTs on the part of non-profit organizations and public institutions is an important but less publicized dimension of the divide. Public institutions and CBOs struggle with access issues; the problem gets worse for CBOs located in semi-urban and rural locations. As we show below, the organizational dimension of the divide – the challenges faced by organizations with respect to ICT access – gets more pronounced as the ICTs get technologically more advanced. Public institutions and CBOs can facilitate access to ICTs and their benefits quite effectively for residents in low-income communities by virtue of their public function. Their lack of access thus presents a two-fold social problem of considerable urgency. ICT access can help public institutions CBOs (particularly the latter) with operational efficiency and fund-raising; lacking access translates to fewer funding opportunities and less operational efficiency. Second, if they lack access, then so do the populations they serve, and these are usually among the neediest groups in a community. These groups lose in two ways: directly, in that they cannot benefit from ICT-enabled innovations in service delivery; and indirectly, from preventable operational inefficiency. Improving organizational access to ICTs is, we believe, a key to narrowing the Digital Divide.

The many, many consulting projects undertaken through our classes have underlined for us and for our students the extent of the need for ICT resources and technical knowledge in the non-profit sector. We cannot do much to help with the first – ICT resources (as we note in Chapter 5, we did run a program as part of CITI devoted to supplying used PCs to needy organizations, but Project CORE, as it was called, had to be discontinued). We can and have helped with the second – access to technical knowledge. Access to know-how is foundational: even to acquire the appropriate ICT resources, buyers need technical know-how. Our students have seen too many examples of organizations getting into "solutions" pushed by some consultant and finding that they had unwittingly tied themselves into non -standard and proprietary systems. Know-how is key to ICT acquisition, planning, use. In fact, know-how is technology in its own right, as some have argued (Mackenzie and Wajcman, 1985).

Over the years, access to ICT resources has improved in our community. A local library, for example, recently received six new PCs from a major vendor; a faith-based coalition received 100 used PCs from a local utility company. However, the lack of know-how is a problem each time recipients attempt to upgrade technology or explore new uses of them.

In the over 250 projects that our students have completed since 1991, the majority of the clients (92 per cent) have been CBOs. LAN planning, design, and installation account for nearly 50 per cent of all needs addressed by our students. For most clients requesting help in these areas, the planned network was the very first in the organization. Internet access is a closely related need and accounts for 35 per cent of all projects. The fact that 85 per cent of our projects so far cover LAN and Internet connectivity shows the magnitude of the Digital Divide as it applies to non-profit organizations. As noted, over 90 per cent of our clients are CBOs. Most CBOs are active at the grassroots level in a community. The services they provide range from senior and infant daycare, support services for disabled residents, youth and minorities, and services in community arts and information access (libraries, legal services providers). A proposal to improve low-income residents' access to healthcare services recently noted the advantages with CBOs as a delivery mechanism: "CBOs are the best-equipped to design and deliver effective outreach and enrollment services...after all, it is the local CBO (that) is the most in touch with the community they serve. CBOs are uniquely positioned to deliver a service that requires a trusting relationship with the target population in their own community"(Greater Springfield Health Access Project, 2002, p. 1.10). Improving CBOs' access to ICTs can improve that of their clientele to resources accessed through ICTs.

This portrait of widespread disparities in access to ICTs and technical know-how was corroborated by the Urban-net planning effort in our community and by the planning efforts in four other communities funded under the same statewide program to develop advanced ICT community networks. The Urban-net planning effort, conducted in 1997 under the direction of the first author, comprised analyses of user requirements, constraints and resources. Two surveys were disseminated among eligible institutions -clustered into eight functional sectors (e.g., healthcare, government, K-12 schools)—and disseminated through the Urban-Net steering committee. The first survey elicited application needs – what users would like to use the network for. The second survey, the longer of the two, elicited details on the ICT and human support infrastructure and constraints at the respondent site. The surveys were distributed to 300 eligible organizations in the community; 85 completed both surveys, for a response rate of 28 per cent. The surveys were followed up with individual and focus group interviews with 45 individuals from 16 respondent agencies, using structured and unstructured questions. The surveys confirmed what we had learned from our consulting projects: LANs were not yet a common technology, Internet access was spotty, and many organizations were struggling with inadequate and outdated PCs; these problems were more pronounced in the CBOs. Sixty per cent of the agencies -both large and small- believed that lack of technical know-how was a "major barrier" or "barrier" to technology planning and acquisition; again, CBOs were much harder hit.

It should come as no surprise that advanced ICTs like broadband and videoconferencing applications can worsen the divide because they are technologically more complex than PCs and LANs. Thus while ICT innovation forges ahead and the corporate sector enjoys the benefits of faster and cheaper solutions, the non-profit sector lags farther and farther behind. We recognize that significant structural inequalities underpin differential access to ICTs and cannot easily be remedied. But locally sourced action to address the know-how gap is eminently possible and urgently needed. We illustrate both the need and the opportunity below with reference to an advanced ICT community network development program.

3. ADVANCED ICTS, COMMUNITY NETWORKING, AND KNOWLEDGE BARRIERS TO PARTICIPATION

Below, we draw on five community network development projects in New York State in order to examine user participation. The Urban-Net was one of these projects. Like the Urban-Net, the other four projects involved broadband ICTs, and their use was restricted to organizations in the non-profit sector ("user" refers to organizations, not individuals.

Generally speaking, user participation in ICT development is desirable for a number of reasons. The resulting system may fit user needs better, and users may accept it more readily because they were consulted. As an analyst once commented with reference to social development projects: "The idea of citizen participation is a little like eating spinach; no one is against it in principle because it is good for you" (Arnstein, 1969, p. 216). However, meaningful participation calls for the availability of necessary resources, and some organizations may be better equipped than others. In the projects discussed below, organizations in general and CBOs in particular faced a number of impediments to participation, such as project delays. Project delays, which were significant in length in some projects and a little less so in others, resulted in planner (participant) attrition and turnover and lack of personnel continuity. Even among personnel that stayed on doggedly, enthusiasm diminished for an effort that seemed to go on and on. The high costs of accessing and using the networks was another impediment; we refer to these as subscription costs below. Such barriers certainly cut participation, in particular by CBOs. We pay particular attention to a crucial barrier – lack of knowledge – in the discussion below.

The advanced nature of the ICTs in these projects biased participation in favor of public institutions who had access to the necessary resources – technical knowledge and support staff in-house – and against those that did not. CBOs and (small businesses) belonged in the second category. Their participation, consequently, was negligible in these projects (small business entities were so small in number in these projects that we dropped them from the analysis). Ironically, these projects were intended to help improve access to advanced ICTs by CBOs and public institutions serving some of the poorest areas in these communities.

We first provide some background on the program that funded these projects. We then describe the knowledge barrier to participation.

In 1995, as part of a settlement of a regulatory case before the New York State Public Service Commission, a major telephone company (hereafter provider) in the state committed $50 million to deploy advanced telecommunications services[1] in economically disadvantaged and underserved areas[2] in the state. As a result of the settlement, a Program was set up to fund development of advanced telecommunications networks in approved zip code areas (we refer to these networks as community networks in the present research). The Program established a competitive request for proposals process to solicit proposals from consortia of eligible organizations for grants, with the term *eligible organizations* comprising public institutions (e.g., city and county government agencies, K-12 schools, colleges, healthcare organizations), CBOs, and small business entities. s. Organizations had to be located in or provide services to Program-approved zip code areas to be eligible for the subsidies sanctioned under the Program. State and federal government agencies were not eligible, and neither were individual residents or households. Two rounds of grants were awarded before the Program concluded in 2000. In all, 22 projects were funded – fourteen urban/suburban, six rural, with two qualifying as urban/suburban/rural combination projects.

Subscribers were eligible for reduced monthly service charges and some financial support toward computer and networking equipment at the user premise (customer premise equipment or CPE[3]). Eighty per cent of every grant went back to the provider to cover costs associated with network infrastructure[4] and services development and deployment. The remainder could be applied toward CPE or incidental training at the subscriber site. Grant funds could not be used toward technical consultants or staff, or for end-user applications development.

The Program's stated objective was to bring "advanced telecommunications services to economically disadvantaged areas of New York State that would not be available in the near future on account of limitations in the advanced

---

[1] "Advanced telecommunications means any combination of network infrastructure and customer premises equipment that supports telecommunications applications beyond those normally associated with standard telephone services" (Program First Round RFP, 1996).
[2] "Economically disadvantaged areas means zipcodes within Standard Metropolitan Statistical Areas (SMSA's) and cities, towns and villages outside SMSA's that are within the operating territory for (the telephone company) in New York State…Median household incomes for the listed zipcodes, cities, towns and villages are below 75% of the statewide median household income" (Program First Round RFP, 1996). Underserved zipcodes were defined as these "where the percentage of households without telephone service is at least 50% above the statewide average…" (Program First Round RFP, 1996).
[3] "Customer premises equipment means inside wiring, physical devices and customer provided software products connected to the network infrastructure in support of the use of specifically designed advanced telecommunications services" (Program first Round RFP, 1996).
[4] "Network infrastructure means electronics, equipment, hardware and software associated therewith, and materials of (telephone company) required to establish connections, either dedicated or switched, necessary to support an advanced telecommunications application within (telephone company's) operating territory in New York State" (Program First Round RFP, 1996).

telecommunications infrastructure and related equipment marketplace"(Evaluation Report, 2001). The Program's definition of "advanced telecommunications services" refers to broadband. Broadband technologies offer transmission speeds of 384 thousand bits per second or above and can support multi-media applications. The project reviewed use newer broadband services such as gigabit Ethernet and asynchronous transfer mode/cell relay services (ATM/CRS).

We tracked the work of volunteer planners affiliated with five projects (Table 1). One of these projects was in our community. These projects – one urban/suburban and four rural – were awarded over $11 million in total funding in the Program's second round. Planners were technical and non-technical individuals representing eligible community organizations. These volunteers had drafted the project proposal and constituted the project steering committee. At the time of the present research, they were representing the community in design and services contracting deliberations with the provider. Many planners were also would-be subscribers to the community network when implemented.

Table 1. Communities and Projects Surveyed in Research.

Project	Program Category	Grant Amount
Central New York State	Urban/Suburban	$3.8m
Western New York State	Rural	$2.9m
Southern New York State	Rural	$1.5m
Northern New York State	Rural	$1.5m
Eastern New York State	Rural	$1.5m
Total Program funding for five projects		$11.2m

A review of the Program guidelines supplemented with interviews with Program authorities suggests the following requirements and expectations of a Program-funded community network.

-   A community-focused inter-organizational network infrastructure linking local organizations and sustained through local knowledge and material resources
-   A catalyst of community development
-   A subsidized provider of broadband services
-   A bridge across the Digital Divide

These community networks resemble next generation metropolitan networks (Ishida, 2000), but with membership restricted to public institutions, CBOs, and small business entities.

Data collection for this research began in mid-1996, with some early network planning steps initiated in our community. Data on the design process was collected in two phases and spanned mid-1998 to May 2000. Planners from all six communities were interviewed in the first phase. In phase two, Program selection committee members and provider staff from engineering, marketing and sales functions (hereafter designers) were interviewed. Our analysis of the development effort in our community ran parallel to both phases of the design research and concluded in May 2000. We draw fairly extensively from our research in our community in the present document.

4. BROADBAND COMMUNITY NETWORKS: TECHNOLOGY AND RELATED FEATURES

The five projects share the following technological and related features.

- *High technological complexity*: These are technologically complex, broadband, open, multi-service and multi-layered community intranets with high-speed Internet access. They can support data transfer at high to very high data rates (1.5 Mbps to 1 Gbps range). The carrier is open to permitting service providers to connect to the infrastructure to provide services to subscribers. These networks are multi-layered, which facilitates service development, transparency and multi-vendor operation. Their broadband nature makes these networks multi-service environments – they can support delivery of high-touch services (high-bandwidth services with rich media content, like video-conferencing) besides information and communication exchange. These networks are not merely logically carved-out locally focused segments of the Internet (Serra, 2000), but rather invert the paradigm: they are "hardwired", broadband, "private" intranets (access is restricted to eligible organizational subscribers) that also connect to the Internet. Relative to dial-up community networks, next generation community networks are technologically far more complex.
- *Costly and complex applications development*: Software applications development for next generation community networks can be resource-intensive and technically complex. For example, the local county library would like to make available its holdings online through a portal accessible over the network and the Internet. The design and development of such a multi-media application (even if piecemealed) with adequate security and service quality assurance calls for complex skill sets and considerable resources.
- *Complex services contracting*: Contracting for services can be complex in next generation community network environments. As their needs evolve, subscribers will be faced with in-source vs. buy decisions on a broad range of telecommunications services, potentially from multiple providers in a competitive marketplace. While this development will benefit subscribers, it will also complicate contracting.
- *High subscription and associated costs*: Network subscription charges (albeit subsidized) range from approximately $300 a month to 15 times that for some high-end ATM services. Internet access and network management charges are additional. CPE capabilities have to be commensurate at the subscriber site, as will the in-house technical support infrastructure: these translate into significant monthly expenses for subscribers. The relatively cheaper digital subscriber line (DSL) service was eligible initially for Program subsidies but was dropped from the eligibility list in 1998.

Planning had preceded design in the communities surveyed. The design process was led by the design staff; planners represented users' interests. User participation in design was not intended. Indeed, the Program's second round RFP directed proposers to specify applications (i.e. how the network will be used), not the underlying technology. User participation evolved as the design process intensified in mid-1999. The reason was simple: the grant was widely seen as a significant community development opportunity, and planners were interested that the network support their present needs and future goals. Every one of the communities surveyed here planned to build on the network through grant-writing efforts. Recall that subscription would not be free. Given the costs of broadband and the nature of the subscriber pool, the design had to be flexible and affordable to attract a range of eligible organizations, and planners were quite sensitive to this.

5. THE KNOWLEDGE BARRIER

Lack of, or lack of access to, knowledge and information impeded participation and independent evaluation of design options. Attewell (1992) documents the critical role played by knowledge barriers in adoption of computing. We extend his insight to user participation in the network design process.

Users need two types of knowledge to participate in design: knowledge about design options and concrete experience with those options (Kensing & Munk-Madsen, 1993). We discuss the first type here; the second is discussed next. Users cannot expect to possess technical knowledge at the level of professional designers, but they need to be informed to participate meaningfully in design. One respondent observed that the more creative design solutions in both first and second round projects had resulted from well-informed planners pushing design staff to explore contextually sensitive specifications. Another respondent explained: "We need information on technology. Why is this surprising…How can we make decisions if we don't know the technology"? Consequently, the most common questions from planners were: How does it work? What can I do with it? How does it compare with other available options? Will it work with what I have now? And, What are the costs?

The RFP's emphasis on applications helped planners focus proposals on what subscribers would do with the network. However, "technology specifics emerged in importance much later", noted one planner. As the design effort intensified, planners struggled in their emergent role as participant designers. They needed knowledge of and "objective" information about design options, from sources independent of the provider. One community had rejected a design proposed by the professional design staff because they felt they were unable to independently evaluate it. According to the county data processing head who wrote the proposal and led the planning in this community, they (i.e. the planners) were "clueless" on how to proceed on their own. They felt they had lost control of the design process.

Users' knowledge shortfalls were pervasive, and concerned the backbone, access (which connected the subscriber to the backbone), CPE, and applications. Planners also had questions about the ins-and-outs of the contracting process for technical support services.

- Backbone: The provider had picked Cell Relay/ATM over SONET as the backbone technology. Gigabit Ethernet was seen as an extension of the backbone. Planners were unfamiliar with Cell Relay/ATM and SONET. Gigabit Ethernet was being deployed in only one of the communities documented here (ours), and this would be the pioneering deployment of this technology in the provider's entire service area, which covers many states. This technology was new to planners and, to an extent, the provider as well.
- Access: Cell Relay/ATM and gigabit Ethernet were also access options. The Cell Relay/ATM services (1.5, 45 and 155 Mbps) prompted questions on costs versus performance, particularly in relation to gigabit Ethernet. As they learned on the job, planners' design concerns broadened to include aspects of the backbone to the extent these impinged on monthly charges. For example, under an initial design proposal, a gigabit Ethernet subscriber would also have to buy an ATM connection to the backbone because the provider was unlikely to support Ethernet on the backbone; this design was subsequently modified to eliminate the additional ATM connection.
- CPE and interoperability: The overall question was: Would these newer technologies work with legacy technologies on the subscriber premise? What edge devices (devices that translated between one technology and another) should one buy? Would they qualify as CPE or infrastructure? Who would manage it? Some planners felt they did not know enough about the access options even to ask the right questions about CPE.
- Applications: High-speed access to the Internet and to shared community databases over the World Wide Web, videoconferencing, and multi-media applications for distance learning, telemedicine and economic development were among the top applications needs in the communities surveyed. The specifics on developing and deploying these applications turned out to be complicated. For example, the relatively new H.323 standard supports desktop video- and data conferencing over the Internet and the LAN. The older H.320 standard for ISDN-based videoconferencing was more familiar to some, but ISDN service was not eligible in the second round. ISDN videoconferencing was implemented through dedicated access; that is, the bandwidth was dedicated to videoconferencing. H.323 users, on the other hand, would have to worry about bandwidth management because access would not be dedicated (that is, H.323 videoconferencing would not be the only use of the available bandwidth). In three of the communities surveyed here, a network of users had developed around the H.320 standard that could be tapped for help; such a help network was unavailable with the H.323 standard. Enabling secure access to data and applications over the community network and the Web called for new controls to be built into systems, and this was daunting to many planners.

Both planners and Program selection committee officials concurred that lack of access to necessary know-how was a critical barrier to participation. Program funding could not be used to hire consultants, and only one of the six communities (not ours) had independent funds to hire technical help. Knowledge shortfalls were acute in CBOs and small business entities and contributed to their relatively low level of participation. Such entities often lacked technical staff in-house. Our planning surveys in our community showed that an overwhelming number of small agencies had no full-time in-house technical staff. One respondent said: "Smaller agencies may be more creative, and may be more aware of what the community needs are. They may not have the technical expertise, but may understand (community) needs better". "In-depth technical assistance" would have helped them benefit from the Program subsidies and make those benefits available to the publics they served, she added.

Not surprisingly, knowledge shortfalls were relatively higher in rural communities. In the urban/suburban communities, shortfalls got steeper the farther one got from the city. Shortage of technical staff in-house significantly affected an organization's ability to participate in the design process.

Knowledge shortfalls had been a significant problem in the first round as well. The first round RFP had asked proposers to specify technologies as well as applications, but proposers were unable to provide this information. A selection committee member observed: "Either they asked for things the carrier (provider) couldn't do, or they simply didn't know what to ask for. There was widespread lack of understanding and knowledge of technology specifics". This had delayed implementation. To get around this problem, the second round RFP asked proposers to focus on applications. Planners were seen as sources of information on applications. The assumption was that the provider would do the design, as it had in the first round, until it became evident that planners wished to participate actively in the design process. The change in focus from technology to applications in the second round RFP may have discounted the need to equip planners to be meaningful participants in design. Program guidelines, by encouraging community institutions to come together and make a case for the investment, had made users stakeholders in the outcomes. But user participation in design had not been planned for. Had it been planned, resources might have been assigned in the Program to inform and educate planners. One planner proposed just this; another felt that a "think tank" of individuals with technical expertise should have been established under the Program for use by communities. Planners themselves emphasized the importance of applications prototyping in education. Given that knowledge shortfalls were a problem in both rounds, respondents felt that applications demos should have been a part of the information sessions hosted by the provider.

Lack of concrete illustrations of design options through prototyping was an impediment, and tended to exacerbate knowledge shortfalls. Planners were frustrated that they could not visualize the network or its uses. Provider-generated stylized network diagrams and flow-charts are useful visualization aids and were used at design meetings. These can be useful early in design to illustrate a technology's possibilities. But they are less useful later, when questions pertain to implementation specifics in actual use settings. Planners felt that working prototypes may have helped answer many of their questions, especially in the later stages of design. Prototyping, or "show-how", can be a powerful complement to and elucidator of know-how.

Applications prototyping can help concretize abstract notions like bandwidth and illustrate the practical value of emergent applications. Planners clamored for access to tried-and-tested uses like the Internet but had difficulty visualizing emergent ones, such as videoconferencing. Projecting bandwidth requirements to accommodate as-yet-unknown uses was, understandably, a significant challenge to them. Applications prototyping can stimulate ideas on use and can be especially powerful in broadband environments.

Based on our experience, two levels of prototyping for show-how are possible: *demonstrations and trials* (the work of CITI in broadband demos and trials is discussed in Chapter 5). Demos are designed to illustrate technology capabilities through generic, sample applications. Our group mounted two live demos of DSL and H.323 videoconferencing over the Internet. The demo focused on technology capabilities. The demos provided "proof of concept" that DSL bandwidth was adequate for high-quality video and audio, and that connecting multiple points for videoconferencing over the Internet did not significantly degrade signal quality. Members of our project group operated the demos, not the user. The demos were informally evaluated on technical criteria.

Trials, unlike demos, are implemented at the user site and may be left there for several months to allow extended use directly by the user with actual organizational work processes. Two sites participating in our trial program used H.323 videoconferencing over DSL for Medicaid benefits certification. The trial was formally evaluated on both technical and organizational criteria, the latter pertaining to consequences of technology use on organizational work. Our trial design roughly paralleled the evolutionary prototyping steps from Thoresen (1993): system sketch, prototype, test and evaluate.

The timing of such interventions is critical. Our demos occurred early in the planning phase. The trial was designed to assist with *design* decisions: How well does the technology perform given my specific needs? Does it work with what I have? What step(s) in a work process can it help with? Apropos, one participant in the Medicaid trial noted:

> Internet (i.e. H.323) videoconferencing is new to us. We are quite familiar with ISDN-based videoconferencing. We have to see how the new system interoperates with legacy systems. Interoperability is important; we do not have extra systems to throw at this. With ISDN, it is like dial-up, it is not on the office network, so it was easy. We did not have to worry about bandwidth issues. But now, with the IP video shared on the office network and needing at least 400 Kbps or so per video stream, we have to look into bandwidth sharing. So far it has not been a problem. But if you are running several sessions at the same time on top of all the office traffic, bandwidth availability may become an issue. The whole world has changed.

Attewell (1992) notes that knowledge is "immobile" and may resist successful transfer into an organization. Adopters often have to grow the knowledge through actual use. "Absorbing a new complex technology not only requires modification and mastery of the technology, viewed in a narrow mechanical sense, but it also often requires (frequently unanticipated) modifications in organizational practices..." (Attewell, 1992, p. 5-6). Trials are more powerful than demos to the extent that they can support learning by doing or learning by using by potential adopters.

Applications prototyping can have symbolic value as well. At most project sites, the long gap between proposal submission and the start of the design process had blunted public interest in the project and contributed to planner attrition. Prototyping efforts can refresh interest in and impart momentum to the project.

The more the use of a network "depends on social organization and mobilization of significant resources, the more it will tend to be controlled by those who are already organized and well-off"(Calhoun, 1998). A recent report by an independent consultant, which reviewed all 22 projects under the Program, reached a similar conclusion: "those institutions already involved in technology and advanced technology such as...community colleges and hospitals were predisposed to or ready to take full advantage of the program"(Evaluation Report, 2001). Continuance of Program subsidies to address the needs of CBOs – "community action agencies, day care centers, Head Start providers, community centers, community health care clinics, legal aid offices, and other service providers located within low income communities" – was recently (and unsuccessfully) proposed before the New York State Public Service Commission (Public Utility Law Project, 2000, p. 3-4).

> Because of the funding constraints which they experience...community service organizations in low income areas are often unable to incorporate...advanced technologies into their operations...By focusing the available rate reductions on this sector of service providers in low income communities...(the continuance of the program) will help bring these customers more directly into the digital economy and bridge the digital divide.

The document continues:

> The non-profit organizations eligible for the reduced rates would include community action agencies, day care centers...community centers, community health care clinics, legal aid offices, and other service providers located within low income communities. By reducing broadband rates for these organizations, real assistance is provided to the organizations which create the social infrastructure on which low income communities depend and, therefore, to the low income families and households which make up that community.

Importantly, besides rate reductions (subsidized network service charges), the document seeks assistance to cover technical support resources and support for ICT resources (like PCs).

6. CONCLUSION

Disparities in access to ICTs are widespread. A commentator notes:

> ...a sharp divide still exists between those who have computers and access to the Internet at home and those who do not...Half the population has the Internet at home. Of course, that means that half the population does not have the Internet at home. It is far too soon to declare victory (Cooper, 2002, p. 225).

The focus of the comment is on individual and household access, but disparities in access even to ICTs that for-profit corporate entities take for granted – such as

PCs and LANs – As we showed, the problem may not go away even when programs specifically targeting the ICT needs of have-nots are set up. What then can we do to address the problem?

The first step is for institutions of higher education to function as mediating institutions between ICTs and non-profit organizations. Mediating institutions

> come into existence where technology knowledge is scarce and/or organizational learning around a technology is burdensome. These…institutions specialize in creating and accumulating technology know-how regarding complex, uncertain, dynamic technology. They "stand between" a user and complex technology (hence "mediating") (Attewell, 1992, p. 7).

University-based outreach programs would do well to emphasize for their students the macro-social relevance of such a function. Such a function could be purely instrumental in its concerns and help adopters to make better decisions about ICTs. Enlisting college students in such an enterprise helps train ICT professionals in the process. A socially-sensitive interpretation of such a function would attempt to go farther by stimulating questions in the learner on the deeper reasons behind, say, disparities in access to ICTs and technical know-how. Why are certain sections of society behind? What can be done to help correct the imbalances? These questions point to a social structural consideration of inequalities and to a politically activist understanding of the mediating function. These questions promote thinking on the macro-social relevance of professional action in the learner and are taken up in the concluding chapter.

CHAPTER 4

EVALUATING LEARNING

1. INTRODUCTION

Active learning experiences require careful monitoring and assessment in order to (1) make sure that learning goals have been met and (2) provide information for making decisions about future active learning experiences. This chapter describes a series of evaluation studies that were conducted to determine the impact of the Community and Information Institute (CITI) projects on students, faculty, and non-profit agencies. Data were collected using questionnaires, interviews, surveys, and case studies. Results are reported and a set of conclusions and recommendations are included for those wishing to incorporate active learning technology consulting projects into their academic programs.

2. IMPACT OF ONE COURSE

Since CITI's inception, a number of different courses (e.g. Systems Analysis, Telecommunications Projects, Project Management) have participated in active learning technology consulting projects in the non-profit sector during the past three years. Our first evaluation study examined one of those courses and the impact of active learning technology consulting projects on participating students and agencies.

"Instructional Strategies and Techniques for Information Professionals" is a graduate-level, semester-long (15 weeks) elective course in the School of Information Studies at Syracuse University. The course attracts students from all three of the School's master's degree programs in Information Management, Library Science, and Telecommunications & Network Management, as well as students from the School's doctoral program in Information Transfer. The course is designed for students who will eventually design and develop instructional lessons and materials related to information skills/technology, assist in the selection, acquisition, and assessment of educational and information technologies, integrate technology into instruction and learning. advise on current trends in instructional media and technologies, and/or provide instructional technology leadership and support. It is particularly appealing to students who are pursuing a career in which the instructional role fulfills an important and/or major function (e.g. information systems manager, reference librarian). The integration in the course of students from different academic programs has resulted in a rich synthesis of backgrounds, experience, and perspectives encompassing systems, management, and service. Course content includes:

- Front end analysis techniques
- Instructional, motivation and learning theories, models, strategies
- Teaching/training methods
- Presentation/delivery techniques
- Evaluation methods

One major assignment requires each student to design, develop, implement, and evaluate an instructional lesson and support materials (e.g., job aids), delivered in class with the other students acting as learning audience. A weakness of the course was the lack of "real-world" experiences. Students practiced teaching each other but had no "authentic" audience with an actual training need.

In the fall of 1997, the course was redesigned in order to participate in the active learning technology consulting projects offered by the School's Center for Active Learning. The course instructor had two instructional goals: (1) to provide a learning environment in which students could apply what they were learning to real-world problems (corresponding to the first learning in community element: opportunities for client-centered work in natural settings) and (2) to empower students to use their newly-learned skills and knowledge in a spirit of volunteerism and community service (corresponding to the second and third elements: providing apprenticeship learning through participation and social context of professional action).

The major assignment, as revised, required students to work in teams to provide needed technology training (ascertained through a needs assessment exercise) to a non-profit agency. Each student received two grades for the project, one based on performance and determined by the instructor and one based on contributions to planning and delivering the instruction as determined by the rest of the team members. The latter was incorporated to encourage active participation by all team members and corresponds to the fourth element: designing the project task.

Kolb describes *affectively complex learning environments* as those emphasizing the types of experiences that exemplify what it is actually like as a professional in a particular field being studied. *Behaviorally complex learning environments* emphasize the active application of knowledge and skills learned to a practical situation. *Perceptually complex learning environments* emphasize relationships among conceptual understanding, information seeking, and problem solving. Through the active learning technology training projects, the instructor was able to integrate all three types of Kolb's (1984) complex learning environments into this course. Students took what they learned in class and in the course readings and immediately applied them to these projects.

Students were matched with non-profit agencies with specific technology training needs. In the classroom, students were provided with a solid foundation in the theory and methods of designing, implementing, and evaluating instructional presentations and materials, as well as opportunities to practice methods and skills through in-class exercises with feedback from both the instructor and the other students. Outside of the classroom, student teams were required to meet with clients to assess training needs and technology requirements, design appropriate training interventions, develop evaluation mechanisms, deliver one or more training sessions, and create related support materials such as training manuals and job aids.

During the first session of the course, representatives from several non-profit agencies in the Central New York area presented their organizations' training needs to students in the class. Following the session, each of the 24 students in the class was required to select one training project, with a minimum of two and maximum of four students per project team. Seven different projects were selected; for example, one project required instructing the staff of a child care agency on how to use a newly-installed email system, another project required the training of social workers from the county health department how to create and use spreadsheets.

Teams were required to meet with their agency liaisons over the first few weeks of the semester to (1) determine the scope and content of that agency's training needs, (2) establish dates, times, and locations of training sessions, and (3) identify and describe those who would be trained. In the following weeks; a portion of each weekly class time was devoted to learning and applying relevant concepts and techniques through a variety of presentations and activities. During this time, the instructor assumed two roles (as specified by Kolb, 1984): (1) *teacher* of essential information and skills and (2) *facilitator*, providing a framework for the learning experiences through information meetings and classroom seminars. In addition, the instructor implemented both of Wagemans & Douchy's (1991) experiential learning types, building on students' prior knowledge of technology and their organizational and communication skills and incorporating sponsored learning activities such as planning with clients, assessing trainees needs and learning levels, and field testing training materials.

Adler (1994) advocates the evaluation of active learning activities in order to measure (1) the knowledge, skills, and attitudes of students as they develop and (2) the value added by the experience. Therefore, in addition to assessing learning through the quality of course assignments and classroom exercises, the instructor administered pre- and post-project questionnaires in order to explore students' perspectives on the impact of the active learning approach on their knowledge, skills and attitudes. Once all projects had been completed, a questionnaire was also sent to the agency liaisons to determine their opinions of the quality of the training delivered, the type and amount of interaction between agencies and student teams, and suggestions for improving future projects (Small & Venkatesh, 1998).

2.1. Pre-Project Questionnaires

During the first class session, 21 students completed the pre-project questionnaire (three students enrolled in the course after the first class session). Approximately one half (11) of the students reported previously participating in at least one active learning technology consulting project (e.g., building a database for a public library, designing and compiling a citizen satisfaction questionnaire for a police department) in another course or activity (e.g., internship). When asked to describe their personal level of involvement in working with the non-profit sector, five (24%) indicated high level of involvement, four (19%) reported some involvement, and 12 (57%) said they had no involvement.

Students were then asked to state their expectations (with the option of selecting more than one) for the active learning experience in which they were about to participate. More than half of the students (11) anticipated having real-world experiences, working with real people and solving real problems. Six students described the experience as one that would be personally satisfying or fun. Two students expressed the hope that the techniques learned would be transferable to other settings, three expected regular feedback from the instructor, and two thought it would be an opportunity to share knowledge.

On a scale of 1 (unprepared) to 5 (fully prepared) to participate in the training projects, students were asked to rate five types of skills. Mean scores indicate that, in general, students felt most prepared in organizational skills (3.9), followed by communication skills (3.7) and leadership skills (3.5). Students felt least prepared in technical and training skills (2.9 each). Most students worriedly believed their training audience would have a high level of technical background (higher than the students), which proved to be quite different from the actual situation they would face. What they discovered was, rather than everyone being at a high level, their learners often represented many *different* levels ranging from total novice to quite proficient. This meant that they would have to design training that accommodates these different levels. Follow-up questions revealed that although most students had some misgivings about their current technology and training expertise, they expected to develop the skills they needed to be successful in their training projects.

When asked about their experience with working in teams, all but two students (91%) indicated either some or a great deal of experience. This was not surprising as the School of Information Studies' policy is to, where possible, incorporate team activities into every course. The students indicated two common concerns about working in teams. The first was whether there would be a balance of effort put forth by all team members. For example, one student stated, "My biggest concern is that sometimes in a team situation, you have one member that is a slacker and slides by on the achievement of others. This can destroy the morale of a team."

The other concern was related to the amount of time/scheduling required for team meetings and training sessions. One student expressed it this way, "With each person having different work/life schedules, I'm worried about finding a time for everyone to meet and to set up a time with the organization." The instructor addressed both team-related issues by (1) providing class time for team meetings with the instructor available for consultation, (2) regularly monitoring each team member's participation in the project throughout the semester and factoring it into that individual's final grade, and (3) asking each team member to assess the participation of all other team members after the training project was completed.

2.2. Post-Project Questionnaires

All 24 students in the class completed a post-project questionnaire. When asked if the active learning projects had enhanced their learning of course content, all students replied in the affirmative, citing the relevance of such experiences. Some comments were:

> It was great to have a chance to apply the class content immediately. It made the course material more relevant and increased my confidence in a group training setting.

> The demands of an external real-world customer made us work twice as hard to learn our materials, implement relevant teaching strategies, and fine-tune our presentation.

> By working with real clients we have not only taught material but learned to negotiate and make adjustments to the experience.

Students were asked to describe the highlights of working with a "real-world" client. Their responses reflected a variety of perspectives.

> Real world" situations have "real world" problems that we had to address. If we were only working with our class, we would not have had the same experiences. There were compromises to be made, schedules to adjust, and various learner abilities to adapt to.

> The most satisfying aspect was learning the content (new to me) and designing instruction that we knew was really needed. We also were happy to leave well-designed products that we know will be useful to many others with our client.

> When you finally start to "click" and see where you're going and feel you understand the need and can work towards it.

> To see the workings of a government agency and the people who made the experience positive.

> The actual training was rewarding after all of the preparation...wrestling with the clients needs and being flexible.

> Feeling that our job aids would really help them in the future.

> That the clients I assisted would become a part of my information network for future contact.

One question addressed students' previously-stated concerns (team member effort, sufficient time) and whether those concerns influenced project outcomes. The two responses below indicate opposing opinions about the time issue:

> My original concern was time. We tried to make the most of our class time since we all had very busy schedules. We tried to divide up the work fairly evenly and were very supportive of each other. I think our group worked very well together. I was unsure of how the group would function but it worked out fine.

> Time restraints kept us from doing many things we wanted to do.

> Knowing from previous students of (the instructor), what the levels of expectations are. I had the mindset that (the instructor) would accept nothing other than top quality work. Therefore, I knew the time and energy would have to be at its peak. It really paid off! There was no room for "slacking" or "putting-off." I am very happy with the outcome.

One student mentioned a different time concern but found it to be a positive, rather than negative, force.

> We were influenced some by time constraints. Our client doesn't move very quickly and wasn't hurried by the fact that the semester is ending. This has given us a little extra time to fine-tune our project and to observe the other groups, so it should be to our advantage. Our client does seem to consider our project very seriously, which has helped us keep it very professional.

Ability levels became a concern after students discovered the range of knowledge and skills held by their learning audiences, as indicated by the following comments.

> The ability of the (learning audience) was the major concern. With the many ability levels, keeping the pace of instruction on target for all (learners) was a concern. By having the extra teachers (other team members) this made pacing possible.

> The large number of potential learners. Once we established a reasonable number of learners and training sessions, it was easy to plan. The other concern was computer experience of learners. It was hard to group them appropriately to make the learning effective.

One team had a unique concern; the successful completion of their training project depended on the completion of the installation of a new technical system by a technology consulting team from another course. Coordination of the two projects became problematic.

> Working with (the team from the other class) was very difficult. We tried to rely on them to help us determine our content and to help us with learning the (software) program. They were basically uncommunicative. Not very cooperative. This aspect of the project was very frustrating.

> Concerns about what would actually be installed and when and not knowing any definite answers until close to the end of the semester. It was frustrating to deal with, but in the end the project itself was not affected..

The most difficult challenge reported by 1/3 of the class (eight students) was the inability of their clients to define and clearly articulate their training needs and describe their learning audience. Although often frustrating, this turned out to be a valuable learning experience for students. Here are some of their comments:

> Client was unsure of what he wanted.

> Difficulty of getting hold of client made it difficult to really begin as we had to wait for points to be clarified and questions to be addressed.

> Client not clear about what was wanted.

> We had concerns about even doing our project because it took us so long to effectively communicate with our client.

> Communication with the contact person – because it took so long to connect with the right people, it was hard to know exactly what we could start on or how far we could work.

> The content need as described the client was somewhat vague. We were forced to work very hard at deciding what to teach in order to maximize our limited time. We also got some mixed messages from the two individuals who were our contacts. It forced us to keep up attempts to communicate and clarify issues.

> Our client was also having difficulties within the organization. Therefore, she sometimes portrayed the learners to be unmotivated or resistant to training.

Some students offered useful suggestions for helping to facilitate trainer-client communication. Some of them were:

> I suggest a contract between clients and students – a more detailed (in writing) description of the need up front with a final "contract" spelling out details (which could be a course requirement) at a later date. This may eliminate some wasted time and "wheel spinning."

> It might be stressed to (the clients) when they make the commitment that we have a definite time limit that we have to meet.

> Perhaps making sure that the client (liaison) is the best contact representative for a particular agency or have.

Students benefit far more from learning experiences in which they are actively involved and self-directed, rather than passive observers. Keller (e.g., 1987) specifies four criteria for motivating instruction; (1) it is *interesting* to students; i.e., capturing and maintaining their attention and curiosity, (2) it must provide *relevance*; i.e. content and activities area valuable and meaningful to students, (3) it operates at the appropriate level of challenge and difficulty in order to build and maintain students' *confidence* in their own capabilities and, (4) it is personally rewarding and promotes learning *satisfaction*. All four of these criteria were addressed by the active learning projects.

Students were then asked to rate the importance of the same five skills they rated on the pre-project questionnaire in achieving success with their training projects. Results indicate that communication skills and teamwork skills were rated most important (4.7 each), followed closely by training skills (4.6) and leadership skills (4.3). Students indicated that technical skills for which they felt least prepared when the project began turned out to be the least important for the success of the project (4.1). Instead "people skills" appear to have been more critical attributes for success.

Students were then asked to rate the importance of the same five skills they rated on the pre-project questionnaire in achieving success with their training projects. Results indicate that communication skills and teamwork skills were rated most important (4.7 each), followed closely by training skills (4.6) and leadership skills (4.3). Students indicated that technical skills for which they felt least prepared when the project began turned out to be the least important for the success of the project (4.1). Instead "people skills" appear to have been more critical attributes for success.

The final two questions asked students (1) if they felt the satisfaction of achieving their personal learning goals and (2) in what ways the community service aspect of the project affected their learning motivation. Their comments reflect all four of Keller's criteria for motivating instruction. For example:

It gave me a way to learn more about and work with an organization that has held much interest for me professionally. If I have time I may offer to provide additional training sessions to the organization because I enjoyed it. (interest)

It was more interesting because I felt the institution was interested in our project and we were doing them some good. (interest)

Definitely more valuable. I have always been interested in doing community-based internships and integrate them into my coursework. (relevance)

Yes. I feel that I learned useful, proven teaching methods and was able to apply some of them in an actual teaching session. (relevance)

Yes, because I wanted to feel I served the community and I have to a slight extent and I feel the ideas learned in class were put to good use. (relevance)

Working with people who had a real need and knowing I was providing a service rather than just completing a project for a grade made this experience much more meaningful. As a result, I got/learned a lot more from the course. (relevance)

Yes, I had more confidence and was more relaxed in a group training session than I've ever been before, It was great to know that our group could work together to create a great training session. (confidence)

An outside community service made the class more challenging, yet rewarding when finished.(confidence/satisfaction)

Yes I did. I personally have established a great relationship with our client. I feel like I have led my group in some areas, and that we have developed a satisfying final product. (satisfaction)

I learned how to teach computer skills. That is very important for my future work. (satisfaction)

It's nice to feel like you're giving something back to the community – especially since many times they would have trouble affording training from a "professional" organization. (satisfaction)

Personal satisfaction of providing a service (satisfaction)

I don't think the fact that it was a community service made any difference, except that perhaps it felt good to be able to do something for someone else. (satisfaction).

The research described above indicates that active learning technology training projects have made a short-term qualitative difference in the learning and attitudes of the students who participated in them. Tornatzky (1983), however, asserts that research on diffusion of innovation has traditionally focused on short-term impact on individuals and advocates that we begin to focus on broader, more long-term effects. Therefore, an attempt was made to collect information that would identify some of those more lasting effects. Three further studies were conducted to determine long-term impact on both students and on the non-profit agencies they served.

2.3. Agency Survey

A brief written survey was mailed to the agency liaisons. The survey contained a range of questions pertaining to satisfaction with the performance of the student consultants. All seven agency liaisons responded to the survey.

The first question asked liaisons about the success of their projects and whether their expectations had been met. Five responded that the projects met their expectations, while two stated the projected exceeded their expectations.

Liaisons were then asked to describe the highlight of the training projects. Their responses were:

> The highlight was observing the students training our teachers in Web page design and having the positive feedback.

> The training materials that the group developed. They were outstanding and – with minor modifications – I'll use them when I offer the class in this coming semester.

> They were a wonderful group – knowledgeable, patient, flexible, and very helpful.

> The product they developed exceeded (my) expectation.

> I was very impressed with the team's enthusiasm and energy. Everyone was willing to listen to new ideas and to adjust to the learners' needs.

> The actual training.

> The outcome. The students provided good "basic computer skills" for the (learners).

Agency liaisons were asked to rate the overall quality of training provided, which reinforced the main learning goal of the course. On a scale of 1 (low) to 10 (high), the agencies rated the training quality high with a mean score of 8.7.

3. IMPACT ACROSS STUDENTS

An electronic questionnaire was administered to a selection of twelve recent graduates (both undergraduate and graduate level) who had participated in a variety of CAL-sponsored active learning technology consulting projects and activities through different courses and independent studies during the past three years. Eight completed responses (75%) were received. Some had participated in multiple active learning technology projects over the years while others had only participated in one such project.

Students were asked to describe any active learning technology projects in which they had participated and what role(s) they played. Responses included:

-   Designing a wireless network among three non-profit agencies
-   Training in Microsoft Word
-   Advice on telecommunications hardware
-   Managing a videoconferencing testbed

- Analysis for an internal email solution

Seven of the eight respondents reported that the project(s) they had worked on had been part of the requirements for a course they were taking. One stated he had participated as a volunteer. The range of agencies for whom the students completed their projects included the Greater Syracuse Tenants Association, Catholic Diocese of Syracuse, Spanish Action League, Onondaga County Department of Social Services, State University of New York Health Science Center, Southwest Community Center, Crouse Substance Abuse Treatment Services, JOBS Plus, and Bishop Grimes Junior/Senior High School.

All students reported having worked on a student-managed team. They were then asked how successful that experience had been and what they learned from it. Comments were mixed regarding the experience, as represented below.

> How to take the lead without simply doing all the work or doing it my way.

> I learned that most of the other members were poor communicators.

> Two of us worked quite well together. The third member did not contribute as much nor did this person put in as much work.

> Deadlines are important; coordination among the members is necessary; motivation is important; work distribution helps a lot.

> It has been very difficult to integrate the academic learning experience of the student team with the professional consulting expectations of the clients.

> ...(W)e were able to coordinate our efforts..

Students were then asked about their expectations for the project and whether those expectations had been met. Some students described their expectations in terms of problems they had experienced while others described personal goals. For example, one student complained that the project description the agency provided had been unclear from the very beginning and they had to rely on their professor's readings on computer networking to guide them through the project. Another said she had hoped to do a good job of training. Another stated he hoped to "gain experience with leading edge technology consulting while contributing to the Syracuse community.

Some reported disappointment in not being able to meet the expectations they had set. For example, one student stated she couldn't possibly achieve the project's objectives because it depended on the installation of donated computers through Project CORE and those computers had not been delivered and/or installed in the time frame available for the project to be completed. Another described his project exceeded beyond expectations and that the client "wanted more." Another student expressed great pleasure that her project had been so successful, stating it had given her an opportunity to research and consult professionally with industry and academic leaders. Still another reported a mixed degree of success:

Expectations were not met in the beginning as the solution provided was not the best but there was success in the end as we did come up with a solution that was economically feasible, required none of the hardware installation, and no maintenance cost.

Some of the most revealing questions asked students to describe what they had learned about working with the non-profit community, including the benefits and difficulties of working on a real-world project. Several responses referred to budgetary and other limitations that affected the success of their projects:

- Shoestring budget
- Lack of time
- Lack of formality
- Client relies heavily on others for equipment and service
- Limited staff
- Lack of technical knowledge
- Fewer IT resources
- Politics

Others revealed some "epiphanies" that had occurred while working with the agencies, such as

- How technology could be of great use (to the agency)
- How "in need" nonprofits are
- The importance of setting clear boundaries upfront to avoid false expectations

Benefits of working on real-world projects evoked the following comments:

It gave me real-world experience.

I can say I worked as a consultant.

It was more than practice. It was an actual lesson.

Exposure to problems, experience, values of teamwork.

Hands-on technology and management experience.

Practicing skills with real-world problems.

Attracts/facilitates networking with the most talented (School of Information Studies') students.

Opportunity to work with industry and academic leaders.

Students described several benefits of working with non-profits, such as:

(They were) easy to work with.

Learning about a different business culture.

They truly appreciate your help.

Ability to share what I learned.

Client had great need for our service.

(It was) easier to communicate with clients as they have more time relatively.

You see what kinds of problems they confront.

Personal sense of contributing to community services otherwise unavailable.

Some of the difficulties of working on real-world projects included:

Trying to meet/exceed client's expectations in three months.

Trying to change people's minds.

Nothing is guaranteed. Anything can happen.

You can never over-prepare.

Coordinating schedules to meet with client and plan with team.

Gathering information, pursuing vendors for information.

Dealing with real people concerns and needs that you may not be able to.

Balancing project and academic responsibilities.

Managing client expectations regarding professionalism level of students.

Managing personal expectations of other students.

The difficulties of working with non-profits seemed to focus on resource constraints and unrealistic expectations of agencies as to what students could accomplish, as revealed in this comment: "They expect more than you are willing to give." Some students also expressed the need for more time: "Need more time to understand clients" and "Need to get to know more about the trainees."

Students were asked to describe the project outcome(s). Outcomes included:

-   Word processing training
-   Researched, documented solution with three options
-   Started them on learning to use computers
-   Training to get them acclaimated to computers
-   Intranet VPN (Virtual Private Network) solution for connectivity of two corporate LANs
-   Installation of end-to-end videoconferencing system with training
-   Recommended appropriate technology

One question asked students if working on the project(s) had enhanced their learning of course concepts. All but one of the respondents indicated it had. Learning outcomes included client management, technology skills, preparing lesson plans, evaluating clients, presenting materials, and project plan design. Some comments were:

> We had to use course concepts right away. Course content was integrated with practice.

> Class knowledge applied directly to practical, real-time problem.

The negative response included this comment, "In this case, no. The (agency) was not advanced enough for the technology discussed in (my) course." Students were then asked to describe what, if any, impact their project(s) had on themselves and on the agencies they served. Some responses included:.

> This project has helped me become a more seasoned professional consultant. While supplementing the theoretical classroom experience, it has also made me more critical of the educational curriculum. I've begun to feel that the (Information Studies) curriculum isn't as technical and up-to-date as it needs to be.

> Being able to participate in this project and having a successful outcome made me feel good about my presenting skills. This experience also made me realize how much you can accomplish if you know how to communicate well with others, that not only you have to know what you are talking about but also how to say it so it can be understood.

> I enjoyed this and would like more experience in consulting for non-profit organizations.

> I think the project was a very positive experience for the non-profit agency because they were able to improve their skills in using Windows 95 and Microsoft Word 97 with a few sessions. They also realized that it was not as difficult as they thought and that with some help everyone do the job better.

> Gave (agency) leaders, some of whom had never use a typewriter, a start in using computers, doing flyers to announce their meetings… which could help to strengthen their organization.

> It may be too early to measure, but it certainly has exposed both agencies to a cutting edge technology. Unfortunately, research involves a large degree of trial and error, which is not the preferred modus operandi of most functional agencies. We have tried to manage expectations and minimize disruptions to normal business processes, but haven't always succeeded.

The final questions asked students to suggest ways in which the projects and the process by which students participate in them could be improved. Some students expressed frustration at the lack of current and potential future resources.

> On both sides, it was difficult because the (agency) really does not have enough knowledge about the potential of their current system. If there had been a person with more knowledge, we probably would not have been needed. The (agency) may look for help again. They are struggling to remain competitive and although in some ways (their agency's services are) better, the (clients) are losing out because the technology resources here are poor.

One respondent talked about the lack of a space for her team to conduct training at the actual agency, forcing them to use a University facility to deliver technology training.

> For the agency members, it would probably have been better if the training would have taken place in their own working environment. For us it would have been easier if the University of the School had a room …available to provide a quality service to the agencies.

Finally, one student stated that his long-term, broader project required more resources from CITI and mentioned the communications difficulties that may arise with international students and clients.

> As the project matured, it really required the resources of a full-time manager, which CITI has been unable to provide given (their) current budgetary constraints. Having a full-time manager for (our) project would significantly improve progress toward expected outcomes. Real-world projects require more input from students than typical academic-only projects, given the expectations of clients. Students should be made aware of this. Additionally, these consulting projects require intense communication between the students and clients. This oftentimes has created complications for non-native English speaking students as well as clients and the projects, in general.

4. IMPACT ACROSS STUDENTS

Two faculty whose courses had participated in active learning technology consulting projects provided information via an electronic interview. The first question asked the instructors to explain why they first decided to involve their classes in active learning technology consulting projects. Their responses reflected an enthusiasm and commitment to this type of teaching and learning.

> When I heard that this option was available, I jumped at the chance to include my students in such projects. Until then, my students had only been able to try out their newly learned skills on each other. This provided an opportunity to use their skills and knowledge with real people who have a real need. This was much more meaningful and exciting for me and for them. I also firmly believe in the concept of service learning and the importance of giving back to the community.

The next question asked instructors to describe what resulted from this participation.

> Incorporating active learning technology projects has resulted in higher relevance of the concepts and procedures I was teaching. This increased student motivation and satisfaction. Students were able to immediately see how the skills they were learning worked and the impact they had on trainees. Learning was reinforced and strengthened as a result. I have learned to incorporate more time for team meetings and feedback from me concerning their technology training projects. I have also included the concepts of active and experiential learning into course content. On a personal note, I have learned a lot about working with the not-for-profit community. Their needs are so great and they are so appreciative of anything you do for them. It is very gratifying to see a win-win-win situation for students, instructors, and agencies.

We asked the instructors to share two or three memorable anecdotes related to student participation in these projects. One anecdote demonstrates one of the potential pitfalls of working in teams, even with graduate students.

> There are three projects I remember most clearly but for different reasons. The first I remember because of a particular student. The technology training project was for an agency that provides services to the local Hispanic community. The project's goal was to teach word processing and spreadsheet applications to the agency's staff. One of the team members was an international student from Venezuela. When I attended one of their training sessions, I observed that student taught in both English and Spanish and translated for her teammates, when necessary. She also produced a professional-looking job aid – a mouse pad that had all of the critical software commands in English and in Spanish. It was very impressive. The second project I remember because of the project itself. The training team provided basic computer literacy and word processing training at a residential group home for abused women. The training took place in a room so small that we could all barely fit. It took place early on a Saturday morning. I remember one woman brought her teenage son to help her and another came in a bathrobe and slippers. A third had to leave from time to time to check on her small children. But they were excited to learn! It was inspiring to the students and to me. The final memory was not a pleasant one. It involved a team of five students (I quickly learned that teams should be no larger than three students). As the semester proceeded, I began to hear grumblings from this student and that about others on the team. Soon it became out-and-out war, where some students refused to talk to others on the team. I began to get email and voice mail messages from distraught students, accusing the others of being slackers or deliberately sabotaging the project. My only recourse was to call the group together and "read them the riot act." It was unpleasant for both the students and myself but it worked. They came through with excellent training sessions that were well-received by their agency. These students will never be good friends but I think they learned a lesson in professional behavior. It was definitely an example of how personalities can negatively affect teamwork and, without intervention, can potentially destroy a project.

Finally, we asked faculty for their "Top Ten Tips" for colleagues who might consider incorporating these types of active learning technology consulting projects into their courses. Here is a compilation of their responses.

(1) Ascertain the status of technology capabilities each agency has before allowing a training team to sign up.

(2) Work closely with the CITI-type organization. They know the agencies and their liaisons and can act quickly when problems arise.

(3) Provide ongoing feedback to teams on their progress and the quality of their work throughout the semester.

(4) Have realistic expectations about what can be accomplished within the time constraints of the academic semester and the resource limitations of the agencies.

(5) As backup for technology training projects, find an off-site location for training (e.g. a campus computer lab) in case one or more agencies does not have an appropriate facility.

(6) Keep teams small (3-4 students). This helps eliminate interpersonal conflict and facilitates communication and progress. Make sure you are aware of what is happening in terms of student-student interaction throughout the project so that, if necessary, you can intercede to save the project.

(7)   Students must have adequate knowledge/skills to be able to successfully complete projects. This may require additional teaching or facilitation on your part.

(8)   Provide an opportunity for students to "show off" the results of their technology consulting projects. We devote the last class session to presenting projects, invite the agency liaisons to attend, and provide refreshments to make it a more festive event.

(9)   Notify the CITI-type organization of any difficulties with particular agencies or agency liaisons. CITI can then try to alleviate any problems or possibly remove the agency from consideration for future projects.

Although these data help us to understand the impact of active learning technology consulting projects on students, there had been no systematic research investigating their effects on the non-profit agencies, the people who work in them and the people they serve. For example, the diffusion of innovation literature indicates that certain individuals within an organization will be "early adopters" of new technology, and their influence will, over time, persuade others to use the newly available technology. Subsequently, a study was undertaken in the spring of 2000 in order to explore the impact of active learning technology consulting projects on participating non-profit community organizations. The purpose of the study was to assess the impact of student-managed, active learning technology projects on the organization and individuals within each organization. This research combined interviews, questionnaires, and case studies to explore long-term impact of CITI technology projects on organizations, employees, and clients in the non-profit sector.

Of the 32 participating agencies over the past three years, fifteen agreed to participate in the study. Agencies that did not participate declined because the original liaison had left the organization and there was no-one else who could provide the information needed.

4.1. Research Questions

This study explores the impact of technology consultation and implementation on non-profit agencies. Research questions include:

(1) Has the introduction of new technology and knowledge into an organization affected how work is distributed and conducted within the organization?

(2) Are there changes in work-related processes at the organizational and individual levels?

(3) How has technology empowered the people who work at these organizations and those they serve?

(4) What further needs (both organizational and individual) emerge as the result of the implementation of technology?

4.2. Methods

Thirty-two agencies in central New York State were identified as having had CITI student projects over the past three years. Each agency was contacted and asked to have someone familiar with the CITI projects participate in the telephone survey. Of the 32 agencies, there were only fifteen in which someone who knew about the project was still employed by the agency.

A series of telephone interviews were conducted with participants from fifteen agencies that had sponsored active learning projects. The participating agencies ranged from small organizations to large multiple-agency organizations within central New York State. They included schools, libraries, a childcare service and education center, a hospital, an organization that places disabled adults in jobs, an environmental education organization, an adult literacy organization, a church, a grief counseling agency, a labor organization, and an organization that provides transitional living services.

An interview protocol was designed, tested, revised, and administered to fifteen agency employees who have acted as liaisons or coordinators for CITI projects. In order to collect the richest data possible, the interviews used open-ended questions, encouraging respondents to tell "stories," describing their perceptions of impact. Demographic and other quantitative data were collected through a questionnaire administered to agency officials. In addition, one agency was identified for more in-depth study. Those interviewed ranged from executive directors to information technology staff, to library directors, school administrators, and clergy.

The number of active learning technology consulting projects in which the agencies participated ranged from one to four and covered a variety of technology needs. Most projects focused on systems analysis and systems design but there were also Web-related, process analysis, and technology training projects. Some examples are:

- Database development
- Feasibility study about providing Internet service to the community through some of the churches
- Evaluated needs and chose the best email package and installed it
- Y2K compliance testing
- Evaluated future needs and present knowledge and then provided Internet training
- Developed agency's Web site
- Set up a computer lab
- Design and set up network
- HTML training for teachers and staff
- Demographic study of Onondaga County
- Word processing and spreadsheet training for clerical staff
- Installing and setting up a LAN

In addition, ten agencies reported receiving PC's and other computer hardware through Project CORE.

All respondents indicated that most, if not all, employees within their organizations use technology. When asked to describe the role of technology within their organization, responses included email between employees, send files to and from funding agencies, maintaining a directory of donations and donators, producing publicity materials, writing reports, for financial records, healthcare, Web site development, learning to use technology in teaching students, and maintaining a database of organizational information. Respondents were asked to describe exactly for what types of tasks technology is used in their organizations. Responses varied including searching online catalogs, communications, spreadsheets and databases, word processing, teaching and tutoring, Web browsing, diagnostics and therapeutics, research, computer-based presentations, patient care, and HTML authoring. Technology users range from staff to administration to clients.

Most agencies considered themselves low to medium in terms of technology use. Three characterized themselves as high tech. Here are their explanations:

> Compared with other non-profit organizations or independent living centers, we are definitely high tech; other independent living centers seem to have a lower quality of technology.

> Many employees use the available technology to its full extent, but many don't. We're trying to let the early adopters adopt the technology and do some informal training with the later adopters so that they will come up to speed on their own time, but will do it eventually. Of course, then the early adopters will have moved on to new technologies.

> (We) have been using computers and databases for several years now for these sorts of databases, but only recently have we gotten the approval and funding to set up an in-huse LAN and a Webform entry to these databases.

The remaining interview questions explored if and how the active learning projects had changed the way work is done in the organization, how are tasks done differently, what capabilities employees have that they didn't previously have, how people's work has changed, and what further projects might be needed to have an impact on the organization.

(1)   Has the introduction of new technology and knowledge into an organization affected how work is distributed and conducted within the organization?

Active learning projects seem to have made at least some difference in the way work is done in all of the participating agencies. Some of their responses are:

> The training and the technology has changed the thought process; we have a different perspective on how to approach or accomplish something. (The network) definitely improved the agency's ability to share files.

> There has been a big impact on all the users – patrons and staff. For the patrons, it gives them an option to produce a decent (e.g. competitive) resume. Similarly, the students can create nice-looking college papers. We will be offering Internet classes, too. Particularly in the inner city neighborhoods, the people do not have Internet connections. This will completely change the type of services we offer.

For the staff, there has been a huge impact on the way we spend our work time. The staff has to help the patrons who use these computers.

Before the donated computers, (the director) would come in early and do her computing in the morning before the office manager (on whose desk the one computer sat) would arrive. Now she can work in her own office, close the door if she doesn't want to be disturbed – she can control her own work setting and environment. Before the Web site was developed, (staff) got many more phone calls about programs and directions, which took up a lot of the office manager's time. They still get these calls, but fewer.

Publicity materials (flyers, brochures, mailings) used to get created by hand or typewriter; now it is done in Word. Directories of members, donations, etc. used to be maintained on paper and in files; now it is done in Excel.

(The projects have) enabled (the agency) to track outcomes of programs and services, collaborate with other organizations to offer services. "Connectivity equals collaboration." Also has enabled emailing of grant proposals to funding agencies, problem requests to tech support, and information to our board of directors.

Files (e.g. medical records) can be emailed to affiliated organizations instead of being sent by mail. Some of the affiliated organizations have Web-based databases and (we) can enter or retrieve data from this as needed.

The LAN and Web-accessible database will change how we work...now, our funded agencies must fill out forms about outcomes and spending and mail them to use and our staff must then enter this data into our databases. In the future, the agencies will be able to fill out these forms online and the data will get entered into our databases automatically. It will save our staff a huge amount of work.

(2)   Are there changes in work-related processes at the organizational and individual levels?

Several agencies reported that a number of tasks are performed differently as a result of the active learning projects. For example, one respondent stated, "We now have a grasp of more of what we have. For example, we now know the exact number of volunteers we have. We are better at doing our financial reporting." Another replied, "Office staff (is) using a database to maintain records of programs and services rather than paper. Tutors teaching with laptops instead of just books. Board of directors using email to communicate with each other." One had a somewhat humorous reply, "More people are utilizing the Internet, instead of playing Solitaire!"

Respondents reported that there are several tasks that can now be done that weren't done before.

We (now) give formal (technology) classes to patrons.

Email between staff members.

People have requested time to use the computers. They are using it and asking to use it in their job when they didn't before. For me, I see that more of them want to have computers on their desks. This gives them the freedom to learn on their own.

Office manager maintains the Web site (with occasional help from the student who originally created it). (All staff) do more writing (grant proposals, publicity, etc.) at the office, instead of at home as they used to.

We are able to track in more detail. For example, a donation can be brought up on the database, whereas before we had to write everything down manually in a ledger book. It also helps with out mailings and we have saved a lot of money in that too. We can easily see if people have responded to our mailings and if they have not in a number of years, we can easily remove them from the list rather than wasting more postage sending them the newsletters.

Email internally and externally. Sharing data on the Web with collaborating organizations. More adept users help the less technologically savvy to use their computers and applications in the absence of formal training.

(Our organization) used to contain many "silos," where knowledge would be in the heads of many individuals in different departments, often duplicating information and how to do tasks. Now with email and file-sharing, silos are breaking down, allowing more collaboration across departments..

(3)   How has technology empowered the people who work at these organizations and those they serve?

We asked participants if the people in their organizations had more or less work as a result of having technology. Nine reported they have more work. Here is a sample of their responses.

We have more work but are able to do it in the same amount of time. We have a very computer literate staff.

Certain people definitely have much more work, like the person who manages the LAN – all the technical aspects and the security.

More now, because the staff and pastor are still climbing the learning curve of using the computers. When they have learned what they need, probably no more work than before.

In some ways it is more work because we're doing more tracking; however, more work gets done in less time.

Always more. Informal training has become an unofficial task of the early technology adopters. And the late adopters have more work just to learn to use the technology.

The teachers have more work to teach themselves to use the technology well enough so that they can include it effectively in their lesson plans. Same for the administration, except that it's not lesson plans, it's just everyday office use. The students probably have more work for the same reasons, but most seem to take to it easier.

Two respondents reported somewhat less work for some people as a result of the active learning projects. Three participants found the workload was pretty much the same after the projects. One stated, "Same amount, roughly, just it's performed differently. Technology has not changed the workload – the amount of available money from the state and collaborating organizations changes the workload." Most respondents indicated that the technology projects did not cause a change in responsibilities of most employees. One explained, "Too few people to shift jobs/responsibilities around. Technology is not integral to the work but it is a tool that makes certain jobs easier."

When asked if technology has made any or all of their staff more productive, most enthusiastically agreed. One responded, "Yes, I get things done in less time. I am more productive" and another stated, "Very definitely! Now one person can do the job previously done by two. Yes, job is easier and more enjoyable."

(4)　　What further needs (both organizational and individual) emerge as the result of the implementation of technology?

Several respondents projected potential future changes to their organizations resulting from the introduction of technology. Some thought there might be changes in the way people do their work. One commented, "Yes. Especially when the LAN is in place. Then there can be real intra-office file sharing rather than the current sneaker-net. Also more resources can be offered online." Another stated, "Already more people are taking personal responsibility for doing research and using the computers." One more said, "Yes. In the long run more will be Web-based and automated, and push technology so there will be less need to run around after files and client information that is needed. It will automatically come to (our organization) when a new client is referred from another organization."

We then asked interviewees what additional technology and/or technology projects they would like to have provided. Most responded they need more and/or faster technology (e.g. higher-end PC's, databases, networks) and training (e.g. spreadsheets, databases, Web authoring). When asked what real or perceived barriers exist in their organizations that might prevent this from happening, common answers were lack of planning, not enough funding, no in-house technical expertise.

5. CASE STUDY

One agency was selected for more in-depth study. The agency chosen was the local branch of a national organization based in central New York State that serves adults with literacy needs and teaches ESL (English as a Second Language). It is funded through the parent organization, the United Way, and through grants. The agency has hosted three active learning technology projects, including network upgrading, receiving four donated 486 PC's through Project CORE, and a subsequent network upgrade.

The agency's entire office staff consists of four full-time employees (literacy tutoring services depend exclusively on volunteers), including:

(1) The Executive Director, who oversees all the others, maintains contacts with other affiliated agencies, the national organization, and the board of directors, writes grant proposals, etc.

(2) The Receptionist, who takes calls from potential students and tutors, & enters their basic data (name, contact information) into their database (LiteracyPro). She also creates flyers, mailings, etc.

(3) The Head Trainer, who provides the (evening) workshops to the potential tutors (18 hours, mandatory, 3 times/year).

(4) The Technologist, who basically fell into the role of "office techie" because she knew more about computers than anyone else, but has no formal training. She also maintains contact information in the database.

Every employee has a Pentium on his/her desk. These are not the PCs that were donated by Project CORE, which donated four 486s. Of these 486s, two are used by volunteers, when they are in the office, and two are not used anymore. All six PCs in use are connected to the client-server LAN in the office. The Technologist maintains the Windows NT server and an 8-port hub. One of the CAL projects installed the wiring for the LAN.

There are two main groups with whom the organization maintains regular contact: the students and the tutors. The process of contact is the same in both cases:

(1) The Receptionist takes the initial call: the person is either in need of a tutor, or is interested in becoming a tutor. The Receptionist takes their contact information and enters it into the LiteracyPro database.

(2) If the caller is a potential student, that contact information will include their requirements for training, location, and schedule of availability. The student is then asked to come in for an interview, at which he or she will meet with as many of the employees as possible, and his or her needs will be assessed.

(3) If the caller is a potential trainer, the Receptionist sends him or her a survey form that includes data about their skills, access to computer, as well as training, location, and schedule of availability.

(4) When this form is returned, the data is entered by hand (by a volunteer, if one is available, usually a student) into LiteracyPro. The potential tutor is then contacted about the next training workshop session.

(5) After the potential tutor takes the training, he or she is a full-fledged tutor. The organization then pairs him or her up with a student. The criteria for pairing would ideally be the tutor's skills and the student's needs, but are usually location and schedule of availability.

The LiteracyPro database is the center of all activity. While they do use the Microsoft Office suite of applications, QuickBooks, email, & Netscape, LiteracyPro is where they maintain all of their information about their students and tutors, who after all are the reason for organization's existence in the first place. LiteracyPro is used for:

- Maintaining contact information. All of these data are maintained electronically in LiteracyPro, from the first phone call contact. No paper records are kept of contacts, except for what is generated as reports.
- Generating lists and labels for mailings, and email addresses for those who have email access (estimated 28 out of 100 tutors).
- Generating reports for the board, the United Way, NY State Board of Education, the national organization, and other funding agencies: reports are generally of student progress and outcomes, and demographic information. (Every agency has its own requirements, so they must change the format of the generated reports accordingly, which is a hassle using LiteracyPro.) Reporting generally happens every 6 months or so. In the future they want to be able to generate reports on the average length of time a student has to wait before getting connected with a tutor, but they do not have that capability yet.

LiteracyPro is the only application that is installed and run off of the server – thus all employees are sharing the same database. All other applications are installed on each PC individually.

The respondent indicated she wants to set up scheduling software on the network. All students must come in for a needs-assessment interview. Currently, this is done using a desk calendar on a desk, centrally located in the office. Since the office is so small (two rooms: the Executive Director's office, and a larger room with three cubicles), this can be done simply by asking the question out loud: "Is everyone available at such-and-such a time on such-and-such a day?"

The agency is not satisfied with the current database software because it does not suit their needs very well. However, they believe that if they configure it too specifically to their needs, the vendor will not be able support it, since it will no longer be the product as sold. They are hoping that the next version will solve many of their current problems, but do not know when it will be released. They would like to move over to a more generic, configurable database application, but none of them know enough about databases to set it up to suit their very specific requirements, including forms for data entry and reporting formats. Additionally, and perhaps worst of all, exporting data is difficult, and they cannot do it in a way that would make it possible to import it into a new database application: therefore they fear that switching applications would require them to manually re-enter hundreds of records into the new database.

The agency also uses other standard applications, including:

- Word processing software used for writing memos,
- Grant proposals, reports, etc.,
- A spreadsheet application used for maintaining spreadsheets of financial and funding information,

- Presentation software (used rarely), for creating presentations for the board of directors, funding agencies, etc.,
- An email system for communication and for participation in listservs (currently only the Executive Director is subscribed, but she is encouraging the others to subscribe),
- An accounting and bookkeeping application, and
- An Internet browser for surfing the Web, mostly for research on other literacy programs and for seeking new ideas, such as new potential funding sources. The agency's long term technology goals are:
- Laptops for tutors, for a proposed "Tutors With Computers" program: Give every tutor a laptop that he or she could bring to tutoring sessions, & literacy software applications as teaching tools. They are hoping to get laptops eventually through Project CORE or other donation, but the Executive Director has found that corporations are willing to donate desktop PCs, but not laptops.
- A portable projector that can be hooked up to a laptop (they do have one, a PowerBook) or PC, for making presentations: to the board of directors, funding agencies, etc. (They already have PowerPoint as part of the MS Office suite.)
- Image editing software for mailings, etc.
- Scheduling software running on the server for scheduling student interviews.
- A computer lab for tutors and students to use individually or together, which could also be used to evaluate literacy teaching software applications.
- Webcams for tutors and students to meet virtually and for the organization to conduct meetings with the tutors and with its board of directors.
- A Web site that provides general contact info about the organization, information about upcoming tutor workshops and registration forms and literacy teaching software applications.

This agency is fairly typical of the small non-profit organization. It has few employees who perform many tasks. It is resourceful in how it obtains technology and other needed resources. It is fairly atypical, however, in that it knows what it doesn't have, what it needs, and dreams about the future and how technology could further enhance its services to its clients.

6. CONCLUSIONS AND RECOMMENDATIONS

A series of studies were conducted to evaluate CITI projects and identify ways to improve both the education of students and service to the non-profit community. An initial study looked at just one graduate-level course in which students were required to provide technology training to non-profit agencies. A second study elicited responses concerning a wider range of students participants who had worked on technology training and technology consulting CITI projects. A large-scale study investigated the impact of CITI projects on 15 agencies that received them. An in-depth look at one agency resulted in a case study. Finally, interviews were conducted with two faculty participants.

Data from these studies lead us to the following major conclusions and recommendations:

Conclusion: Communication between student teams and agency liaisons is critical to the success of a project.

Recommendation: Communication can be facilitated by a mediating organization (such as CITI) by providing structure and guidelines to faculty (for students) and to agencies.

Conclusion: Agencies have limited resources that often inhibit the breadth and scope of projects.
Recommendation: CITI could maintain a database of each agency and its current and anticipated resources. This information, available to both faculty and students, would help all parties to set realistic expectations for their projects.

Conclusion: There are a number of potential constraints when working with the non-profit sector.

Recommendation: Describe some of these limitations in the course syllabus so that students are aware of them before starting to work on projects.

Conclusion: In addition to cognitive knowledge, students learn skills and experience in teamwork, project management, and client-consultant communication and develop a sense of pride that the results have added value to a number of social programs and services offered within the community.

Recommendation: Make students aware of these potential outcomes in course descriptions and syllabi.

Conclusion: Technology consulting projects appear to have a positive impact on the work processes and capabilities of the non-profit agencies who participate in them.

Recommendation: Make agencies aware of these potential outcomes in CITI's promotional materials.

*The authors wish to thank Jeffrey Pomerantz and Pamela Revercomb, doctoral students in Information Transfer in the School of Information Studies at Syracuse University, for their assistance with the research reported in this chapter.

CHAPTER 5

IMPLEMENTING THE EXTENDED MODEL OF LEARNING

1. INTRODUCTION

The Center for Active Learning (CAL) – which at present serves as the vehicle for learning-in-community projects for our students – was established in response to a need. The demand for consulting help from public institutions and CBOs in the area had increased significantly since 1991, when the idea of learning-in-community was first tried out. Student demand for hands-on ICT consulting opportunities had grown as well, so much so that it made sense to develop some kind of formal structure to administer the growing number of projects. Looking back now at the path that led to CAL and CITI, it seems as though it almost created itself. The flow from conception to realization was surprisingly quick.

Chapter 3 raised the *Why* question: Why learning-in-community? Why now? This chapter addresses the *How* question: How did the organizational forms – CITI, CAL and later additions – came about to implement the learning-in-community program? We present the development of these forms in chronological order, starting with the steps that led to the CAL.

In most professional fields, providing students with practical skills to complement theory is a prerequisite to certification for practice. In disciplines such as medicine, it would be unthinkable to offer a curriculum that did not have a practice component. Fields of study in engineering and applied science also have strong practice requirements. It is expected, and is increasingly a differentiator among programs, that high quality academic courses of study in the professions include direct, hands-on application of theoretical knowledgeunder the supervision of a senior practitioner. This is the standard model of learning and credentialing in the professions.

The systematic study of ICTs and their use in organizations is well suited for such a model and indeed; most quality curricula offer significant opportunities to students for hands-on learning. Student demand for direct work with ICTs has also grown. With the growing proliferation of ICTs in the home, K-12 schools and the workplace, more and more students are entering college with considerable technical knowledge and direct experience. These students want more than just a theoretical understanding of how things work. They are looking to gain proficiency and concept mastery through hands-on work with ICTs. Increasingly, this interest centers on ICT consulting work. The appeal here for learners is the multi-faceted nature of such work. Effective ICT consulting calls for a mix of technical, social, and managerial skills. Because it is multi-faceted, teamwork is the norm. Learners eager for such experience are told to brace themselves for high levels of ambiguity and complexity as they learn to deal with the technical and social challenges. We discussed the challenges involved in Chapter 2 under *planning* and *design* work. Hereafter, the term *ICT professional* refers to the trained individual whose understanding of both the technical and social (we include here the managerial as well) aspects of ICTs facilitates a thoughtful approach to problems and opportunities in organizational environments. Consulting is a natural corollary of such a function. Our learning-in-community program is consistent with such a construal of the ICT professional's organizational function. The types of organization served, of course, is restricted to public institutions and CBOs.

In looking at how best to prepare a student in terms of the learning-in-community model and in line with quality professional training in ICTs, we considered methods from other disciplines. The medical internship provided one method. University-level ICT programs routinely offer internship opportunities to students. At the School of Information Studies, the internship method has been in existence for many years and has been very successful. Given the aims of our learning-in-community model though, the experience would have to occur in the non-profit sector in the proximate community. Such environments usually do not challenge interns the way large corporations can. For-profit businesses are more attractive to interns for a number of reasons: they usually have well established and well funded ICT shops and technical staff and thus provide a good learning environment; the experience is valuable "resume material" and may open the door to a full-time job offer at the same site or from a corporate site elsewhere. Non-profit environments lack these advantages: their ICT shops may be (and very often are) outdated and hodge-podge; the technical staff is meager in size and overworked, with little time for training interns. Non-profit sites also often lack the prestige of corporate sites. This is not say that such sites do not have their appeal for interns, but it cannot be characterized as universal.

Another approach considered was the case study. This has the advantage of being based on real world problems, and it offers faculty a good measure of control on what is learned and how. Its obvious limitation, of course, is its abstractness. The case may be a superior simulation of an organization's social ecology. It may depict the players and the climate vividly and in rich detail. But the portrait is fixed; it is static. Real ecologies are fluid and changeable. They cannot be predicted in advance. They feature power wielders and turfs and competing cliques. Case studies have their advantages and can be powerful teaching and learning aids. But we needed a method that was more concrete.

We combined features of the internship and the case study with the principles described in the last chapter to evolve the approach we have used with the class projects. The key term is *evolve*: the approach has evolved over the many years we have used it. We have relied on feedback from students, participating faculty and clients to make adjustments.

The immediate challenge was to make the non-profit environment attractive as a learning environment. What if students had to work on real problems of consequence to the client in real organizational settings? It is here that the task motivational principles discussed in the last chapter came into play as we thought through this. Our very first client was such an environment – a K-12 public school (this experience is described in detail below). In going back and reviewing this experience at the end of that semester, it became clear to us that giving the student (i.e. the student team) the responsibility to make decisions and manage the project for an identifiable client was a promising way to offset some of the limitations of non-profit environments stemming from their lack of ICT-resources. We realized also that the lack of ICT resources was actually a motivator by underlining the scope and size of the client's needs and that of their opportunity to make a difference in real terms.

The case study method suggested some additional possibilities. A student coming into the class with professional work experience could be directed to a project to test some of her "theories" relating to ICTs development and use in organizations. The client site doubles as an informal site for "theory-testing". A student who had interned in a large corporate office wanted to compare ICT purchasing decisions at a public institution. She signed on for a project (with two other students in the class) that gave her the opportunity to study purchasing decisions at this site. On occasion we have selected project sites to illustrate emerging ICTs. A nursing home served as a site recently because of its interest in video-based applications and broadband telecommunications. This worked quite well, but we use such criteria only occasionally. For the most part, clients select themselves by getting in touch with us.

2. KICKING OFF LEARNING-IN-COMMUNITY: THE INAUGURAL PROJECT SITE

Student evaluations for the first author's Spring 1991 Information Networking class indicated a high interest in hands-on learning. The course was at the intermediate-level and presented ICTs (with a focus on telecommunications technologies) from the technical and managerial perspectives. It attracted senior undergraduate students and graduate-level students from the School of Information Studies' three Masters programs – library and information science, information management, and telecommunications and network management. Students felt that direct experience with relevant technologies would be especially valuable given the abstract nature of the course material. They wanted to be able to ground the concepts by working with ICTs and by working through technology management issues in organizations. Earlier editions of the course taught by the first author had elicited similar comments. It was clearly time to do something about it.

Using laboratory resources and case studies was one way to deal with the need. However, a possible new alternative presented itself over the summer of 1991. A faculty colleague at the School of Information Studies received a request from a K-12 public school in the area for help with planning and designing a school-wide ICT upgrade. This included PC systems as well as the school's local area network (LAN) infrastructure. The school had a high need for such an upgrade but did not have the resources to contract it out or to do it in-house. The school's need was conveyed to the first instructor. Would the *Information Networking* course offering the in the Fall take on the project and serve as a consultant to the school?

The school became the first ever project site that Fall. Thirty-five per cent of the course grade was assigned to the project. Students enrolled in the class would work in teams to provide the consulting service to the client. The class that semester had an even number of graduate and undergraduate students. Five teams with six students each were formed and assigned different topics at the site. The teams were viewed as self-managing entities working under the overall guidance of the instructor, who served as guide and coach on the project.

We learned much that first semester. First, it was clear to us that what had at first seemed a straightforward project was far from being the case. We learned that no project, if one drilled down deep enough, is small. We had started out with the idea that two of the five teams would work on the LAN while the others developed a telecommunications plan for the school. As the semester progressed, we realized that the school's needs were more numerous and our assumptions had to be revisited. Project and team assignments had to be redone mid-course. At the end of the semester, five project reports on as many topics were submitted by the class: one on LAN planning and design, the second on tying the school's mid-range computer (or mini computer, which is smaller in size and capacity than a mainframe and larger than a PC) to the LAN (this proved infeasible), the third on Internet access, the fourth on the school's old wiring plant, while the fifth addressed the overall telecommunications plan.

Second, the school's systems ran off a mini computer that could not be tied into the LAN because of it was too old. The wiring plant was in disrepair and poorly documented. Mid-way through the project, the school wanted Internet connectivity added to the things they needed addressed. The school administration – the principal, vice-principal, the librarian, and the technology manager – was in support of the project, but the faculty and staff had not been kept informed and had no notice of it. The LAN development work (planning, design and installation) promised to be more disruptive than originally envisaged due to the state of the infrastructure, and it wasn't at all clear that the rest of the school was, or had been, prepared for the intervention. The school's technical support staff comprised one full-time person and one technically savvy teacher, who helped out when she could.

A service contract with a vendor (the contract was shared with other schools) supported the software applications. It was clear that LAN connectivity, when implemented, would place additional new burdens on the support staff. No one, including the principal, quite knew how the new ICT environment would be supported. The criticality of the need for ongoing staff and user training, and for acceptable use policies, surfaced in a powerful way.

Third, it was clear that we had to rethink the one semester timeframe. The client's needs would have to be addressed in a phased way, starting with a self-contained departmental LAN and Internet access. LAN-based access to applications on the mini computer would have to wait because the school did not have the resources to make the needed upgrades to the mini and provide support for its ongoing use. The school had not thought about the ongoing use environment – the need for support, access policies – until prompted by the student teams that worked on the project that first semester. The school administrator and the students learned an important lesson about the practical aspects of change initiatives – the importance of planning and of gradually phasing in innovations, the need to think carefully about the implications of new ICTs for existing policies practices before taking action.

Fourth, the experience suggested changes to the design of the field project assignment (as the project assignment was called). The modified version of the assignment emphasized the importance of planning. We urged students to think of ICT planning in the expanded sense of the term, as including problem setting and bounding, and analyses of user needs, constraints and resources. As argued earlier, the planning effort provides the project team with *the* operative criteria for assessing the goodness of fit of the design recommendation.

The team's end-of-semester report must demonstrate this fit. The school's administrators had a grand vision for ICT-enabled excellence in classroom pedagogy and administrative efficiency and effectiveness. This called for PCs in every classroom and office connected seamlessly to the internal LAN infrastructure and the Internet. This plan had to broken up into smaller sub-plans to be actionable. Needs had to be prioritized and evaluated in light of the available resources and relevant constraints. Value decisions had to be made – who got connected first, to what, under what terms? At the same time, the client's vision – the big picture – must be kept in view to ensure that the local solution would scale up. In the project assignment description, we urged students to adopt a five-year planning horizon to emphasize the need for evolution and growth in the solutions recommended.

Fifth, we decided to reduce team size to three or a maximum of four, down from six. End of semester student evaluations and project debriefing sessions – where the teams and the instructor reviewed the project experience – showed that team functioning was hampered if team size went beyond three or four members. We also decided to set aside class time and employ asynchronous means – listservs and group email and later, a class website – to facilitate inter-team coordination. In the school project, the LAN team and the Internet access team had to work with a shared set of assumptions because the technologies were so closely related. Similarly, the wiring plant team and the LAN design team had to work in a coordinated fashion. However, inter-team coordination would increase the burden on teams. Looking back, using class time to effect information hand-offs between and across teams has been a relatively efficient and effective way to handle coordination issues.

The school project resulted in follow-on projects at the school the following semester, when LAN and Internet connectivity were installed. The rest of the telecommunications plan – the wiring upgrade, and integration of the mini computer with the LAN – could not be followed up on due to a change in leadership at the school. In the semesters since, many more projects with public institutional and CBO clients have followed.

Within a few semesters of this initial step, as many as 60 to 70 were signing up for the class for the project experience. The number of clients volunteering to be project sites also grew quite dramatically. Students valued the hands-on ICT consulting opportunities offered by the class. Many liked the fact that their services were only available to public institutions and CBOs.

The initial successes led to expansion of the idea. There were other clients that wished to participate, and more projects resulted. As the number of participants continued to grow, the idea for a formal entity – CAL – emerged as a way to manage the growing number of projects as well as facilitate the inclusion of a field consulting component in more courses within the School of Information Studies. As teams installed ICT solutions at client sites, clients asked for more services, such as database applications, systems analysis, training. Formal organization was needed. With more activity all around, more management was needed. It wasn't practical to have each interested faculty member run their own show. An umbrella organization was needed that could work with clients, students and faculty. Such an organization would provide the administrative support needed to provide participating faculty with a pool of clients and topics, and help ensure that the experience was productive and satisfying to all constituents. Also, importantly, we needed to ensure continuity in the coordination of project work across multiple semesters, and through the summer. These considerations led to the birth of CAL. CAL arose from a need – the need to have a central function to manage all the projects.

At present, partly as a result of our own success, roughly one-third of the project requests seek help with installing solutions recommended by teams from previous semesters. A student team proposes a solution, the client invests in equipment, and then a student team in a subsequent semester is asked to help put the solution in place. This has worked well by and large, but the description of the assignment is modified to reflect this shift in emphasis wherever relevant; the team is not in consultant mode, but in implementer mode.

3. ESTABLISHING CAL

The next big step was the recognition that funding would have to be found to make the idea of CAL a reality. After reviewing the budget of the School of Information Studies, the decision was made to recruit corporate sponsors. It was clear that without a source of outside funding, an active learning entity could not be implemented quickly. Our funding needs were not large; the most pressing need was for a project manager, who would liase between clients, students and faculty and manage the project life cycle. The project manager would be responsible for soliciting projects from clients, matching up client needs with relevant courses and faculty, and assisting student teams over the course of the project on client interface issues. The project manager, as we note below, is a key operational function.

Several foundations for private and corporate giving were approached. The idea was appealing for several reasons. First, it was characterized as an investment in the community rather than a donation. The projects already completed had a value that exceeded their cost. The community at large would benefit not from a handout, but from a better ability to do their work. Because the completed projects supplied proof-of concept, it was not a risky proposition. The university had already started the ball rolling.

The initial funding was small but allowed CAL to come into existence. In a small room donated by the School of Information Studies, an administrative office and a computer lab were created. Two positions were established, the Director, which was honorary, and the Project Manager, which was a paid part-time position. There wasn't much equipment in the lab, but the plan was to buy what was needed with the available funds and gradually build the inventory up to support experimentation with various network technologies and configurations. CAL 's articulated mission was to add value to our students and clients through the field project assignment and other formal vehicles, such as periodic colloquia designed to increase awareness of technology in the public sector and the community at large. Our interest was to help public institutions make informed decisions about ICTs; focused colloquia, we believe, can help clients be better informed clients in our projects, while also increasing their general technical awareness.

CAL is the active learning vehicle within CITI. Managing the field consulting project experience through classes at the School of Information Studies is CAL 's main function. Lessons learned from the CAL experience include the following.

3.1. Legitimacy and Visibility

Make sure you have buy-in from the academic unit for students to sign on for the project experience as part of a for-credit class. In the absence of this, student motivation tends to suffer. We do have a few volunteers participating in our new technology projects for no payment or course credit, but they are in a minority and are usually very highly motivated. Generally speaking, undertaking a project for course credit promotes a higher degree of commitment on the part of the learner. It also positions the course, and the project experience, as an acknowledged part of the curriculum and the academic program, giving it legitimacy and visibility. This helps prospective students – in particular those at the undergraduate level – as well as clients.

Courses in systems analysis in design, database, and user training philosophies and methods at the School of Information Studies have used CAL to provide their students with hands-on project work opportunities. These courses, all at the graduate level, were modified to accommodate the project experience. A fourth course, *Telecommunications Project*, was developed specifically to serve as a vehicle for the project experience. The project is worth 35 to 40 per cent of the overall course grade. The course includes two other, more conventional assignments (based on archival research) in addition to the project, but the project experience is the dominant feature of the course. The course has been offered continuously since it was proposed by the first author in 1997.

Academic prerequisites to courses participating in the project experience have to be very carefully thought through. Students signing up for *Telecommunications Project* should have taken one of these prerequisites: systems analysis and design, database, LANs, and/or introduction to computer networking. This list is quite comprehensive, but there usually can be no guarantee that even students with the same prerequisite will be at comparable knowledge levels. The project is a key element of the course. However, the instructor is forced to review communications and networking foundations over the first two, three or even four class meetings (out of 14 in a semester). This is useful for those that need it, but is redundant for those who are eager to engage advanced topics and get started on the project itself; it diverts time away from project-focused discussions. Ideally, a project-focused course should cover issues centered on project work. Possible topics to consider include appropriate tools such as network simulation for what-if analysis of design options, project tracking and management techniques, and network performance analysis and management tools and techniques. For reasons described in Chapter 3, we feel that this would be the appropriate course to formally address broader social issues surrounding computer access inequalities. As we described in Chapter 2, while work on the project exposes students to such social concerns, we would like to augment such exposure with a more formal reflective component on the social issues themselves. Currently, this is not feasible on account of the introductory technical material covered in the class. Diversity in student background can be beneficial. As we note in Chapter 2, peer learning in teams through peripheral participation can and does occur (our experience is that it is diverse skill types, not skills. We believe that successful network planning and design call for diverse skills in those doing it. Planners and designers need people and organizational skills (critical in user requirements elicitation) as much as they do technical skills (key to good design). "Soft" skills are just as important for the team's own health and well being as they are for that of the project.

The diversity of our classes, and the nature of project work, allows, indeed calls for, the happy and mutually productive coexistence of diverse skills and abilities. However, it is important that there be some uniformity within skill types, so that, for example, students with the systems analysis prerequisite have a similar background within that domain. In an ideal world, this would be a given. In our case, this is a desideratum at this point.

3.2. Didactic Philosophy

We presented an extended model of active learning in Chapter 2, with four focal elements to it: client-centered work in natural settings, project task design, learning through participation, and the social context of professional action. This model guides our practice.

3.3. Liability Issues

Clients need to fully understand that, by being clients, they are helping further the education of students. It is important that they understand this: it relates the work they are sponsoring to larger pro-social issues, as well as protect us from potential liability. We have not had to get formal sign-offs from the client on this, nor have any liability issues come up so far. It is a social contract: the team will deliver to the client what was promised in the project scope statement (which is agreed to during the initial presentation by the client and the instructor in class), and the client will cooperate with the team and facilitate access to organizational information and knowledge resources.

If students sustain any type of injury while engaged in project work, the university's standard provisions provide coverage. What happens when a student team report turns out to be inadequate? About ten per cent of the over 250 projects we have directed fall under this category. A project report may be inadequate for any number of reasons: lack of needed skills or team dysfunction, client distraction or non-availability, project scope change of a significant nature during the project. When this happens, the instructor has to identify the cause and take appropriate steps. If it is due to the client (say due to personal non-availability during the project), the instructor has to consult the client to decide if the project should be terminated. If it is due to the team, the instructor has to decide whether to apply more resources or personally complete the project. If a Fall project is inadequate, a team from the following Spring semester can work on the problem. If a Spring project is inadequate, the instructor has two options: see if the client can wait until the following Fall, or assemble a team for coverage over the Summer under an independent study or internship arrangement. Occasionally, we have had to complete a project or part of a project ourselves. Quality control is critical and can be onerous, and falls to the instructor to enforce.

We have had our share of problems with delinquent clients as well. A small number of clients have pulled out of the project mid-semester for a variety of reasons, leaving the team or teams with no project. This can be problematic, to say the least. The instructor has had to step in and find a closely related problem for the team to work on perhaps with another client or on a simulated basis.

3.4. Project Management is Key

The CAL Project Manager is the primary interface between the center, clients, students and participating faculty. In this key role, the Project Manager is responsible for recruiting clients, conducting the request for proposals (RFP) process, working with faculty the School of Information Studies to identify appropriate classes and projects, scheduling class presentations by clients early in the semester to kick projects off, ongoing liaison with clients, faculty and student teams through the semester, scheduling client attendance at student team presentations in class at the end of the semester, and ensuring that clients get a copy of the student team final report.

A critical element contributing to CAL ' s success is the quality of the project experience for all concerned. It is a challenge for faculty to support an active learning experience through their class because it requires different actions and behaviors from a traditional class. Faculty have to learn to guide and coach, not lecture. They have to be able to think like practical problem-solvers and stay abreast of current developments in the solutions marketplace to provide substantive guidance to students on a broad range of problems. Having access to a network of local expertise can help students find answers to questions in areas outside the faculty member's competence, and such questions are common. For example, a student team could fill no documentation for the wiring plant at a client site; the site wiring design had been done by the executive director's husband, and he had used a non-standard approach and color coding scheme. The team was directed to consult the campus wiring group within network computing to "clean up" the client's wiring. It is unpredictable just what the instructor may have to do to keep student teams on track. How does one help a team that is having difficulty getting the client to meet with them? In situations like these, a good project manager can spell the difference between success and disaster. Faculty who have had a bad experience with a client or a project are less likely to participate again. This is true of clients as well. Students usually participate for only one semester, and it is arguably even more important that their project work adds value, and is seen as adding value, to their degree program. Such problems are better prevented than corrected after the fact.

3.5. Working with Clients

The project manager is tasked with recruiting acceptable clients into the program: (recall that CAL's, and CITI's, focus is exclusively on the public sector and CBOs). The RFP process is one vehicle for recruiting clients, but not the only one. For example, the head of a local telephone company's community affairs program called to see if a public hospital would qualify as a client. Referrals like this one, and from current or past clients, are a steady source of project ideas. Proposed projects must be assessed for suitability (feasibility and completability in the time frame of one semester). The Project Manager helps prepare the client for the project experience and assists them in their project sponsor role. Such assistance, which is provided on an as needed basis, could include helping the client with needs assessment, preparation of the one-page needs description for the class, identifying an appropriate representative to work directly with the team, and helping with project(s) definition.

Managing client expectations falls to all participants: the instructor, the student teams working on site, and the Project Manager. The Project Manager sets the frame when she contacts the client through the RFP process. The typical client is desperate for solutions: they may have some technology, most of which, they'd cheerfully admit, dating back to "antediluvian" times ("belongs in the Boston computer museum" and "prehistoric" are other common descriptors); they have very limited resources, which rules out bringing in expensive consultants; they have very limited technical skills resources. When they get wind of the RFP process, they are eager to believe that the projects would help solve all of their problems, and quickly. This is untenable. But even if it were possible to solve all of a client's problems through the projects in a semester or two, organizational disruption from change of this scale would be hard to support. The Project Manager has to advise the client of such realities, using examples of past projects, problems and success stories to ground the client better in what was possible through the project intervention.

The client is advised that their project may not be picked by students. Note that student teams select the project to work on from the slate of projects on offer that semester; the instructor may occasionally suggest a project to a team to broaden coverage, but this is resorted to only when there are multiple teams vying for the same project while others have no takers. We believe that student motivation is key to project success, and being able to follow their interest is a key motivator. Clients are advised that projects with little appeal may not be selected, and so it is up to them to try and "sell" the project(s) during their presentation in class.

The RFP process starts late in the previous semester or very early in the semester that project work is undertaken. The mass mailing (targeting eligible organizations introduces CAL and its mission, describes the courses on offer in the coming semester and types of projects desired for each course – information designed to help the client develop their proposals. Resources that clients must be prepared to provide are outlined. An alternative to the broad-based RFP approach is the adoption model, whereby we identify one or two clients per semester and "adopt" them – student teams work on different problems for the same client. This approach has its merits. It may be an efficient way to tackle closely related problems. A client may want to host their own World Wide Web server and Web applications. An adoption model would allow the server team and the application team to work together in the same semester. Our typical client often lacks basic infrastructure and financial resources for technology. Undertaking related projects over multiple semesters allows such clients to phase in technology. However, as our clients start to look beyond the basics, we may use the adoption approach.

The Project Manager reviews RFP responses and collates them for faculty review. The selection of projects and clients is a collaborative effort involving the Project Manager and participating faculty. Decisions are based on course requirements and assessment of the client's ability to provide the appropriate level of support for students. Past projects conducted with that client (if any) are evaluated including feedback from students. We have turned very few clients away; more often, if a client's request appears to fit another class better, it is considered for that class if the instructor is a participant that semester. If not, the client is advised to reapply in a future semester. The client is then informed of their status that semester, and their presentation in class is scheduled. Participating clients are required to present their needs in class. Failure to appear for the initial presentation will normally remove those projects from consideration unless other arrangements have been made in advance.

Some clients feel that what they get for free is worthless. They may participate as clients for one reason or another, but shirk their responsibilities. This is a tremendous disservice to the students, and to the class. Clients have to understand that they have responsibilities too. Before coming on board as a client, the Project Manager (and the instructor) has to make sure that the client understands their responsibilities. By signing on as a client, the organization agrees to work with the student team and support student learning via the project, and provide the team access to relevant information, people and other resources in the organization. The organization also needs to designate one of their staff as project contact person; this person helps coordinate on-site data collection activities and meeting scheduling. This person also undertakes to attend the team 's project presentation at the end of the semester in class; this is a key responsibility. The team's final presentation is in the nature of a briefing, and is incomplete without the client's physical presence in class.

Albeit few and far between, there have been instances where clients have failed to meet their commitments to provide support to students. Some reasons for this have been legitimate, such as the illness or departure of a key employee, but others have been less reasonable. For students to receive a quality learning experience, the clients must fulfil their obligations to provide access to the organization, help the team's progress, provide necessary resources (such as making employees available for training sessions, for example), answering questions, and generally facilitating the project.

Examples of the types of problems that have arisen have been: clients missing meetings with teams, clients losing critical resources, clients failing to meet their commitments, equipment shortages or delivery delays that delay the project. The Project Manager has to let the client understand, as tactfully but as firmly as possible, that the project, every CAL project that is initiated, subsumes a social contract between the parties concerned and that the client has a set of responsibilities just as the student team does. Recall that the client is advised of responsibilities through the RFP process and through subsequent interaction before the project is set up. Nonetheless, such problems have occurred after the start of the project.

The project manager's goal is to finish up with a set of projects that meet the goals of the courses to be offered in the next semester or two. Because of the amount of preparation involved and because the university is on a semester schedule, it is wise to plan for the full academic year and not just one semester. Clients should be oriented to this schedule for work completion so that they can plan effectively as well. Following the release of each semester's schedule of classes, a client presentation schedule is established for early in the semester. The practice is to have clients present their needs to participating classes during the first week or two of classes.

3.6. Working with Participating Faculty

Faculty want to include an active learning component in their courses, but hesitate when they estimate the coordination effort that would be required to do so. The Project Manager absorbs this substantial burden. She (CAL 's Project Manager and now, CITI's current Project Manager, have both been women) sits down with interested faculty to explain how the active learning experience works and what it entails for participating faculty. The Project Manager may follow up with them to determine what classes will offer the active learning component and works with them to define the types of projects that will be used for each class. This is usually done well in advance of the semester start.

Once they sign on, the Project Manager extends to the participating faculty member a full range of services – scheduling client presentations, following up with the client through the semester to ensure that the projects are on track, working with student teams through the semester to prevent task-related or interpersonal frictions from blowing up into crises, coordinating client visit to the class on the day of the final presentation, and making sure the client receives a copy (or two) of the student team's final report as soon as they are completed.

The ability to handle exceptions is a key feature of the Project Manager's job. In a recent semester, student teams in the end-user training methods class had signed on to design and deliver a comprehensive training program for several non-profits. These non-profits were recipients of funding from the large, local institution. The Institute (CITI) was developing a software application for this institution to allow funding recipients to report use of the funds back to it. The application was set to go online in six months, and the training class seemed an obvious choice to train the recipients on use of the software. Midway through the semester, however, the institutions decided to go with another package. Training users on our package would be pointless. The Project Manager, and the course instructor, had to scramble to find a suitable substitute project for the teams involved.

A number of CAL projects have involved multiple semesters and classes. For example, a first semester team completes LAN planning and design, followed by a team in the next semester that installs the LAN at the client site. In subsequent semesters, other teams follow-through and install software applications and design and deliver training to end users and staff, while a third team develops a website for the client. A typical project of this sort would involve coordinating teams from classes in telecommunications, data base, user training methods, and Web applications.

For faculty, CAL began by simply providing potential clients and projects. As multiple semester and multiple-discipline projects evolved, a mechanism to provide continuity became necessary. CAL now assists faculty with management of proposed and ongoing client projects including progress-to-date, background information about clients and projects, project tracking across semesters and classes, and planning and coordination.

CAL also handles the administrative aspects of coordinating and scheduling client presentations, screening proposals, and providing coaching and support to not-for-profit management and representatives.

3.7. Working with Students

Student work on projects in self-managing teams. The team is responsible for managing its task-oriented activity as well as its interpersonal climate, and can discipline its members. As such, the team has substantial authority over its own conduct and work. However, the Project Manager has to step in to resolve disputes in the team or between the team and the client.

The team's initial contact with the client tends to color and shape the client's response to the team. Students have to understand the importance of professionalism – punctuality, courtesy, reliability, sensitivity to the client's circumstances, commitment to quality, and professional demeanor -in dealing with the client. The Instructor highlights these values in class, and the Project Manager reinforces them. A professional-looking team will elicit a like response from the client; a dysfunctional team should not expect much from the client. The Project Manager may use the code of conduct developed for use with the School's internship and coop program to advise and counsel students during the project. In a recent semester, a borderline team had trouble meeting with the client. Investigation revealed that the blame had to be shared: the team had been tardy in requesting the first meeting, and the client had not responded even after repeated attempts by the team. The instructor worked with the Project Manager to get the team back on track.

At the beginning of the semester, after the Instructor outlines the project requirements in class, students are advised to review the requirements and decide if their schedule would accommodate the time commitment needed to satisfactorily complete the project. We use subsequent class meetings to describe the project assignment in detail, giving the student lead time to make a decision to keep the course or drop it. With conventional courses, a late drop jeopardizes no one. In a project course, a late drop jeopardizes the members of the team and, importantly, the client. The team may be unable to complete the project as planned; the client may have reduced coverage or no coverage at all that semester. Such problems have to be dealt with on a case by case basis. We have directed the team to refocus the project slightly if a member should drop the course late. In a recent case, two members dropped the class very late, leaving the team with just two members. The project was too large for the two members to undertake. A second team was working on the same topic for the same client, but was understandably reluctant to add the two "orphaned" members at this point in the semester. The instructor had to scramble to find an alternative assignment (a more conventional one, calling for archival research) for the "orphaned" students, and advise the client that one of their topics would not be covered that semester. Such course corrections late in the semester may be unavoidable; fortunately, we have had to deal with very few such cases in a decade's worth of practice.

The Project Manager also helps teams with substantive technical advise on projects. This has occurred in two ways. One, the Project Manager herself had the expertise and shared it with the team. Two, she has directed the team to appropriate resource people for help. The Project Manager's central position in CAL and in the project life cycle process gives her access to a broad-based network of expertise she can tap into when needed. CAL' s own resources have served as such sources. Through the projects, CAL has built a web of informal relationships with the computing staff on campus, the computing staff in area corporations and public institutions, and CAL alumni. Students can work on projects with little risk of failure. They may be doing something they've never done before, but they won't be trying to do something that's never been done before. Whatever technical problems they run into, the answers are available and readily accessible.

At the end of the semester, the clients and students meet in class once again. This time it is the students' turn to give formal presentations of their projects to the class. Students, the instructor and clients come together to discuss their original goals, how they solved problems, and what was delivered. This is followed up with a survey from CAL to the clients asking for feedback on the experience and ideas for improvement. Clients are also asked to give input on students' performance that is factored into their grades. Students are surveyed for feedback on the active learning experience as part of the university's assessment of the program and to provide a continuous improvement mechanism. We have used our own customized surveys in addition to the standard ones to gather data on student perceptions of the project experience. The Project Manager is a central player in the project procedures at semester-end; her work ranges from arranging parking for the clients and ensuring that teams invite their clients for the presentation to helping draft the student evaluation surveys.

3.8. Student team Matters

As noted above, small teams of three or four students work better than teams of six. Each team is assigned a project. Teams pick their own projects. For motivational reasons, the instructor does not assign projects to teams. More than one team is allowed to engage the same project (for the same client); however, each team is expected to prepare its own report. Although they are encouraged to coordinate their data collection activities (so that the client does not have to repeat), they are encouraged to think about the problem independently and present their own conclusions, based on the data. The requirement that each team prepare and defend its recommendation introduces an element of competition, which has so far been productive and beneficial to learning. Friendly competition prompts the teams to work harder.

Each team member is required to assess their own contributions to the project in a note that is attached to the team's final report. The note has to describe the member's specific contribution to the overall team effort; the note may acknowledge members who were particularly effective or otherwise as well. This has proven quite effective in catching out slackers.

The original intent behind the projects had been to provide an opportunity to learners to work as consultants with a real client faced with a real problem or opportunity in a real organization. It was decided to focus the effort on the public and no-profit sector. Public institutions – organizational entities such as K-12 public schools, hospitals, government departments – and CBOs, in particular the latter, are in need of ICT consulting help. Small business units are often just as needy, but we decided to exclude them from our scope for two reasons: we felt uncomfortable making available for free such services to for-profit entities, and the ICT needs of public institutions and CBOs generally are more urgent, and we decided to assign them higher priority. Over 250 CAL projects have been completed in the last decade, benefiting several dozen organizations in the local community. Some recent projects:

- Internet fax server implemented for the Urban Ministry Project, a faith-based initiative to combat inner-city social problems. The fax server is the first in the 315 area code, and will enhance UMP's ability to communicate quickly with community leaders.
- Wireless connectivity between community center and community arts center: Student team planned and designed a comprehensive networking plan for the client and demonstrated wireless solution.
- LAN and Internet access implementation for a county branch library

- Comprehensive network design for the Spanish Action League
- Design and implementation of AS400/LAN integration a public institution
- Design for integrating AS400 with NT/IIS Web server technology for a charitable public institution

4. PROJECT CORE

While the equipment purchase strategy for CAL was still being developed (eventually, we bought the equipment from an online auction house), one of the corporate sponsors offered to donate surplus computer equipment for CAL to process and donate in turn to needy non-profits. Although we had not considered computer donation as part of CAL 's outreach function, it was an opportunity to augment our ICT consulting service. Equipment could be donated to clients to complete projects that were stalled for lack of equipment and client funding, a common problem among non-profit clients. Project CORE (for COmputer REuse) was born.

Project CORE's mission was to integrate, whenever possible, equipment donations with CAL projects. Not all recipients of Project CORE computers have been project clients, but we did give preference to clients who also wanted computers in addition to the technical help from the class. This allowed us to donate computers within the context of projects; teams could implement or try out recommended solutions using Project CORE computers. At the end of the semester, the client would have the team's consulting report plus Project CORE PCs. Students got hands-on experience while the client got an infrastructure, albeit of a basic nature. Coordinating the equipment delivery and the class project at the client site has not been easy. Generally speaking, the PCs have been available but the upgrades have not, delaying the implementation process. Software has been a problem; we receive PCs without any software on them. Owing to licensing restrictions, Project CORE PCs are donated without any software. The client has to purchase the software, and this has delayed projects.

We decided to keep eligibility requirements to a minimum. Organizations with legal status as non-profits (this includes public institutions and CBOs) could request Project CORE machines on letterhead, with a brief description of how they planned to use the machines. The recipient also had to be open to serving as a CAL project site for a student project.

Project CORE accepted all equipment that was offered, despite a lack of storage space. Almost overnight, CAL was bursting out of the room granted to it in the School. There was no problem figuring out what to do with the PCs, but there was a problem trying to store them while they were being tested, repaired and funneled into a myriad of projects. Fortunately, CAL was supported by the university in recognizing the potential of this opportunity and taking advantage of it, and storage space was found. A part-time position was established to manage Project CORE activities – coordinating the testing and fixing of received equipment, identifying and qualifying recipients, coordinating equipment donations with CAL projects, researching cost-effective upgrade options, and installing upgrades with student help.

CAL was quickly inundated with hundreds of used computers – mostly PCs of the 486 class. The donated equipment was only three or four years old, but was being replaced with new units at the donor's site. The age of the equipment was usually not a problem for most of CAL's clients, because although it was not up to the corporate standard, it was better than what was in use at many similar agencies. In fact, before Project CORE, some client organizations had no computing capability at all. In the years since its founding, Project CORE has been a significant success. Over 150 of the neediest CBOs – day care centers, church and youth groups, parochial schools, small public libraries in the poorer sections of the community – have been served through Project CORE. Project CORE computers are not simply donated; they go out to the recipient as part of a package. Project CORE staff clean and certify the machines before they are donated, include information on its strong points and limitations, and suggest upgrade avenues and pricing information; while we don't stock any inventory, Project CORE staff have installed upgrades purchased by the recipient. In 1999, we adopted the slogan "1000 by 2000" for Project CORE; to date, well over 1,000 computers have been donated, well ahead of schedule. At this writing, Project CORE is being wound down for a variety of reasons. Used computers – even PCs of the Pentium class – are getting cheaper and within reach of most non-profits. Applications suites are getting harder to find for some of the older platforms. The sheer volume of work involved in Project CORE made it difficult to support other CAL activities (notably the advanced technology projects). Also, importantly, a waste disposal issue arose because it was discovered that certain units that were donated were classified as hazardous waste and created a potential liability for the center.

The Project CORE coordinator's job is multi-faceted: procurement of equipment, managing donations (from corporate donors to CITI and from CITI to local non-profits), providing technical expertise and know-how for equipment refurbishment, directing the activities of student helpers, and coordinating with the CITI Associate Director and CAL project manager to support both clients and our own in-house projects with technology. The ability to direct students in the repair and refurbishment of donated equipment ties in with the importance of effective procurement. Because equipment is recycled into clients networks or into the CITI lab itself (to support in-house projects), there has to be a good selection of equipment on hand. Through Project CORE, the lab provides an environment where equipment can be tested, repaired, upgraded, loaded with software, and networked for practice and learning. For students in CAL projects, the lab has served as a resource for testing solutions and practicing planned work before trying to perform it at a client site.

5. THE COMMUNITY & INFORMATION TECHNOLOGY INSTITUTE (CITI)

CAL played a key role in the development of the Urban-Net. CAL led the ICT planning and worked with the local telephone company on the technical design of the Urban-Net. CAL 's role in the project spawned projects focused on advanced ICTs and software applications. The projects were suggested by our work on the Urban-Net planning effort and they went beyond the scope of CAL 's original mission. The projects involved cutting-edge ICTs, were estimated to take far longer than a semester to complete, called for a higher level of technical expertise than typical CAL projects, and required significantly more coordination in that they were undertaken in concert with vendors and service providers, who donated resources equipment, services, funding, expertise -to the projects. We refer to these projects as advanced technology projects below.

Three design guidelines framed the Urban-Net development effort: the network would support for the Internet Protocol (IP), which forms the basis of the Internet, it would offer a range of broadband connectivity solutions, from the relatively inexpensive (such as digital subscriber line or DSL) to the more expensive (asynchronous transfer mode or ATM, and gigabit Ethernet) to allow participation by both resource-rich and resource-poor organizations, and it would be designed so that the telephone company managed as much of it as possible. The planning effort had revealed a high interest in multi-media applications such as videoconferencing, in high-speed access to the Internet, and in database sharing.

When the Urban-Net was being planned, potential subscribers did not know very much about DSL or multi-media applications over the Internet. DSL was knew, and there were a number of questions about its performance. Applications like Internet video were new as well. The telephone company suggested that CITI mount a demo of Internet video over DSL to test and demonstrate its capabilities. In 1998, CITI staff designed and set up two live demonstrations, both linking CITI and a local Internet service provider with a public university in the mid-west. The demos were very successful and launched our current program in advanced technology projects. The demos involved a great deal of work. The staff as this time comprised the Director, the Project Manager, and two graduate students recruited to develop the demos working part-time at CITI. The two graduate students assembled a team of students, graduate and undergraduate, from the School of Information Studies to help with the demos. The demos were developed using donated equipment and services. The telephone company donated the DSL connectivity; Internet service was donated by a prominent local Internet service provider; the software and hardware endpoints and backend equipment for videoconferencing were donated by video vendors. The design, installation, testing, and troubleshooting of the demos were done by the CITI team. The successful demos triggered other project ideas in community institutions -such as a follow-on trial of the same technologies at the client site, demos of other advanced solutions like Web-enabled database applications.

Such projects were central to the evolving an informed ICT environment in the community, and were enthusiastically welcomed by students at the School. However, these projects were also outside the original mission of CAL, which was focused on assisting needy organizations with basic ICT decisions while providing students a forum for hands on consulting work as part of regular classes. Under the emerging paradigm suggested by the demos, there was a need, both at community organizations as well as among our more advanced students, for projects involving advanced ICTs. We decided to expand the scope of our mission under the umbrella of a new organization, to be called CITI the Community and Information Technology Institute. CITI was established in 1998 at the School of Information Studies. CAL became a component under CITI focused on active learning through class projects.

CITI was established with three staff members – the new position of Associate Director was created to supplement CAL 's two positions. CITI's Project Manager oversees CAL projects (offered through regular classes) and also serves as a liaison with CITI project partners, funding agencies, and consortium affiliates. The Associate Director works with the Director in grant-writing and developing strategic partnerships, and runs the Broadband Applications Center.

CITI projects are not offered through regular classes for two reasons: because of their technical and coordination complexity, they tend to span several semesters, and, as such, personnel continuity, particularly continuity of leadership, is critical. CITI projects are led by funded graduate assistants or by staff paid on an hourly basis. Project participants could be interns or students doing an independent study under the Director. Project teams are self-managing, autonomous entities reporting to the Associate Director.

CITI's mission spans community action and research. CITI is dedicated to promoting advanced technology use and application broadly in communities through

- Technology transfer and prototyping
- Web-enabled application development
- Education, activism and partnerships
- Social science research and consulting

Through our hands-on community action initiatives, we promote and facilitate access to advanced technology applications and services in public institutions and low-income communities; through our research, we analyze and document impacts of and change processes stemming from the introduction of advanced technology into public institutions and CBOs.

5.1. Technology Transfer and Prototyping

Our work on the demos demonstrated the power of applications prototyping as a way to "open the eyes" of potential adopters to possible applications of advanced technologies. The demos also highlighted the need for a locally based technology transfer function to assist local organizations through knowledge-sharing, prototyping, consulting with high technology decisions. Advanced ICTs are complex, multi-layered, multi-service environments. An adopter is faced with complex technical and technical support services acquisition questions. Payoff is unknown, so risk is high. An adopter needs *know-how* to make informed decisions. We believe show-how – through functional prototypes that show how a technology can be applied and used – is a key complement to know-how and key enabler of technology transfer. CITI's technology transfer mission serves the public and non-profit sectors through a program of prototyping for show-how, and through seminars and colloquia aimed at awareness-raising in the local community.

CITI staff – with student and client participation – plan, design, implement and evaluate the show-how effort. Vendors and service providers contribute equipment and services and reduce cost and risk to the client. All of CITI's show-how projects – small and large – include a formal baselining effort that precedes it and a formal evaluation effort at the end of it. As with our other services, the prototyping service is provided free of charge to the client. Prototyping projects have included the Internet Video Test-bed Project –Internet videoconferencing over DSL for Medicaid/Chronic Care benefits certification screening. This project built on the demos: the ICTs were installed at the client site and used with the client's business processes for up to three months. This experimental video network was used to link the County's Department of Social Services, which administers the benefits certification process, the county's leading hospital, a city nursing home and a human service agency serving the community's Hispanic population. This telemedicine network was focused on an administrative application may expand to include support for clinical and continuing medical education applications. CITI's advanced ICT prototyping program is spearheaded by a specialized unit – called the Broadband Applications Center which is discussed below.

5.2. Web-enabled Application Development

CITI teams have developed a fully Web-enabled, secure database application for a large non-profit institution. Other software development projects under consideration include next generation distance learning and an application for unified messaging.

5.3. Education, Activism and Partnerships

CITI's CAL program was discussed at length earlier in this chapter. CITI's educational outreach targets technology and functional area managers in public institutions, to raise awareness about advanced technologies. Periodic seminars, colloquia and show-how demonstrations and trials have been the vehicles.

CITI is active in national forums to advance the cause of community networking and reduce the extent of the Digital Divide in the US. CITI is a founding member of the New York Advanced Communications Environment (NYACE), which seeks to assist public institutions and CBOs with advanced ICT decisions. NY ACE brings together CITI and two other institutions – New York State Technology Enterprise Corporation and a defense research lab – and covers a broad range of technologies such as DSL, ATM, gigabit Ethernet, advanced IP applications, and broadband wireless and satellite communications.

5.4. Social Science Research and Consulting

Our social science research is closely tied to an activist agenda focused on broadband technology transfer into public institutions and CBOs. We are currently studying broadband community network development, diffusion processes, use and impacts in economically depressed zip codes in our own community (the Urban-Net) as well as five other communities in New York.

6. CITI'S BROADBAND APPLICATIONS CENTER

Our central recommendation to a New York state agency recently was as follows:

> We recommend the creation of a new organization – a new technologies cell within state to implement the continuous learning program by coordinating the transfer of knowledge. This would resonate well with state's (1996) IRM vision. The cell is envisaged as a coordinating entity, which would work with existing state initiatives and technology transfer institutions in the state in implementing the learning program and in systematically disseminating the learning among state technical and strategic planning staff. The cell should focus on lowering knowledge barriers with respect to emerging technologies as well as the emerging services market. It is critical that the cell be given cross-agency oversight so as to be able to coordinate technology investment decisions across agencies, in the interest of coherence. A periodic newsletter and/or a World Wide Web site to be maintained by the cell may be good avenues for disseminating the learning internally as well as for publicizing the state externally as a continuously learning organization.

The Broadband Applications Center grew out of this recommendation. The center, which was established in August 2000 with funding from a major telecommunications vendor. The center facilitates CITI's advanced technologies transfer and applications prototyping program.

The new center's mission is

- Prototyping for show-how
- Applied technical research and development
- New technology evaluation
- Market development for emerging broadband services

Projects include
- Secure Telehealth and clinical telemedicine: Evaluation and deployment of secure access solutions under the Internet Video Test-bed. The clinical telemedicine applications will enable a small town hospital to link to the county's major healthcare facility for pediatric cardiology consultation.
- IP telephony: Implementation and evaluation of Internet telephony (IP telephony) solution for public institutional clients
- Flexible access and next-generation services: Evaluation and development of flexible service selection using layer 2 tunneling over DSL, ATM and gigabit Ethernet access.

7. BENEFITS FROM CITI

CITI benefits all stakeholders. Clients get access to technology in a context that is low-risk for them, because they don't have to expend limited financial resources to purchase it. If they are not technology literate (and many of them tend to be, although the numbers are getting smaller), they get help planning their acquisitions from consultants who are highly motivated and who have no financial or commercial axe to grind. Through the Broadband Applications Center, organizations get an opportunity to "test drive" emerging solutions at very little cost. Clients freely admit that without CITI's assistance they would not have had an opportunity to trial Internet videoconferencing with the Medicaid benefits certification process. CITI's very active applications prototyping and technology transfer program is dedicated to facilitating access to advanced solutions in communities.

Through CITI, students get access to real clients with real problems to solve, and an opportunity to work as real consultants. They come face to face with real world conditions, and learn from interacting with professionals in the field. For example, the Internet video test-bed project ran into a roadblock when the telephone company said they could only link participants over their own Internet service; however, the service would not be activated for many months, threatening to delay the project by several months. A student member of the project team wondered why the participants, all of whom were local, couldn't be linked directly through the DSL device at the telephone company, bypassing the Internet. The telephone company wasn't sure that was possible. The DSL vendor was contacted in a three-way conference call, and the vendor advised the telephone company on how to effect the connection bypassing the Internet. How many undergraduate students get the opportunity to work through problems with pros in the field? CITI's active learning environment provides students with an enriched learning experience. Surveys completed by students suggest that their satisfaction with this type of learning tends to be higher than with traditional methods. CITI allow students to apply in the real world what they've learned in classes and books. Students say they greatly value the opportunity to apply class content while still in school, in a low risk context. Students also felt they learned course material better when they were able to apply it immediately to solving real problems for a real customer. Furthermore, they believed there was value in learning to negotiate, plan and discuss projects with clients. As we noted in Chapter 2, providing a critical service to needy public institutions as part of class work is appealing and very rewarding to many students.

Although the School offers a co-operative study and internship program, the experience provided by CITI is different in that faculty and students have a high level of control over the scope and goal of the learning experience. With internship and co-op programs, what the student learns is often at the employer's discretion. In contrast, the projects sponsored by CITI give control over student learning to the instructor. And to the student himself. As we argued in Chapter 2, CITI projects enjoin client-centered work on the student. As with other learning stimuli, the student is free to "blow it off" (i.e. act irresponsibly), but we have noticed that the presence of an institutional client, to whom they are answerable (not to mention the instructor) makes for a profound difference in the "feel" of a project. The presence of an identifiable client enhances a project's professional feel, its appeal. And students, for the most part in our experience, respond very positively to such appeal.

The School and the university have benefited in many ways. CITI has generated positive recognition from community leaders, promoted student satisfaction and improved town gown relations. CITI projects provide participating faculty an opportunity to stay in touch with organizational use contexts, emerging solutions, practical problems that stem from solutions development and implementation, and vendor strategies. This is an invaluable learning experience for faculty as well as students. Faculty consulting and research work benefits CITI through project and funding opportunities. CITI's work on the Urban-Net opened up many new project and possibilities for our students. The study of ICTs in organizations is as much a practical discipline as it is conceptual and theoretic, and CITI facilitates instructors and students to stay current with developments in the field.

CITI's corporate sponsors include major telephone companies and telecommunications and systems vendors. CITI adds value to corporate sponsors in a number of ways. CITI's applications prototyping work helps develop markets for emerging broadband services. A case in point is the Internet video test-bed project. Ongoing evaluations indicate that both Medicaid benefits applicants as well as the process owners – the county, the hospitals and nursing homes – love the technology and want to see it become part of how the process is delivered to applicants. When this happens, CITI will have helped develop a market for videoconferencing services where none existed before. CITI's Secure Telehealth project through the Broadband Applications Center will prototype cutting-edge security solutions -such as on-the fly encryption of video -for use with telemedicine applications, adding a new dimension to federal guidelines protecting patients' privacy. Our corporate sponsor would be able to add value to customers through our applied research and development and prototyping work. CITI's Internet Telephony project could include the development of special software to enable unified messaging to support a particular widely used email package; this development would enhance the solution's appeal for users of that package. Our ongoing applications work in next generation distance learning promises to add new features to enhance the quality of distance learning and collaboration. CITI's mission to serve public institution and CBOs melds very well with corporations' interest in combining social action with product, services and market development. Corporations recognize that they can reap significant benefits from using projects in the non-profit sector as test beds for new innovations.

Our work enables public institutions – note that, under this label, we include government institutions, healthcare agencies like hospitals and CBOs to try out advanced solutions while exposing emerging products and services to potential new markets. We are vendor-neutral in our technology transfer work. We aim to provide potential adopters with the tools – information, analyses, prototypes -they would need to make better decisions. CITI teams are currently working with the university's systems staff to test and compare two leading Internet telephony solutions. These are complex and expensive technologies, calling for significant skills and time commitment to set up and test. Potential adopters seldom get to test even one solution – not to mention two –before purchase. As part of this project, we intend to assist at least one other public institution with a prototype implementation. It is difficult to overstate the value of such a service for the client. This client, a city government agency, is very interested in Internet telephony for its cost-savings, but has no realistic way to get his hands on a box to try it out Through the prototyping project, CITI will expose the client to one leading solution, but we will also provide comparative information on other leading solutions.

Aurora is a small non-profit that provides sign-language services to the county's sizable hearing-impaired population. The Internet video test-bed project team was faced with a critical question: would Internet video over DSL be able to transmit, at the required speed and resolution, the signing of its skilled staff? Aurora had never used video before, but wanted to test it out as it promised to significantly improve the efficiency of their service delivery by cutting down on staff travel time. With the team's help, Aurora staff tried out the technology and found it to be acceptable for their purposes. Again, should video form part of Aurora's standard mode of service delivery, CITI will have helped make a market, in the process assisting Aurora, a small human services non-profit, to make an informed decision. Also helped would be video vendors and service providers in general. Last but not least, Aurora's questions made for a great learning experience for our students, who had to grapple with encoding and transmission standards as they worked on the problem. As we noted in Chapter 2, prototyping work is a powerful learning vehicle as well for our students. Such work exposes students to a vendor's products; this constitutes "mindshare". Students working on CITI prototyping projects will graduate with a better sense of our sponsors' solutions that that of competitors'. But because our perspective is critical and informed by the imperative to develop knowledge (both for our students' as well as our clients' sakes), and given CITI's avowed vendor neutrality, the intellectual approach we wish to promote in our students (and clients) is that of an informed, demanding inquirer. Interestingly, our vendor neutrality benefits the vendor as well. They give us their best, knowing they will be subject to comparative assessment.

8. THE FUTURE

From a pedagogical viewpoint, the growth of the Internet presents some very intriguing possibilities. Public institutions and CBOs in general are poorly served with respect to ICTs and access to technical expertise. With the explosive growth in the number of distance learners (the School of Information Studies has several popular distance programs) linked over the Internet, it would be possible to design an innovative active learning exercise as part of a project-focused course. For example, teams composed of distance learners in one geographical area could work as consultants for a local public institution. The format of the project assignment would be similar to the one we use with CITI projects (through CAL). However, using distance learning tools, such distance teams could be linked back to CITI as well as connected to other distance teams from the class over the Internet. This would allow teams to compare notes and learn from one another as they progressed through the project. It would allow faculty and CITI staff to provide assistance, tips, access to documentation (e.g., team reports from pervious semesters) and to online expertise from the communities of practice both local and virtual. Periodic sessions over video could be scheduled to bring together teams, clients, faculty and CITI staff for project discussions and quality control. At semester-end, teams present their reports over the network. This is feasible today. Remote teams could set up and test video capability at the start of the project (at a client site or mutually convenient location) and use it to stay in touch (video is only one option, but it can greatly enhance communication). As the School of Information Studies' distance learning population grows, CITI may expand the scope of its project work to include remote learners.

CHAPTER 6

TOWARD A RADICAL VIEW OF PRACTICE

1. INTRODUCTION

In this concluding chapter, we briefly summarize the concerns of the preceding chapters and look ahead to a more radical role for learning-in-community programs such as ours. Disparities in access to ICTs and technical know-how are structural in nature. Efforts to reduce these gaps can be *topical*: they may address these needs by providing ICTs and/or access to know-how. Our program has been topically focused in this sense. Alternatively, such efforts could be politically active and represent the have-nots in resource allocation decisions. The latter role is more *radical* insofar as it seeks to address power imbalances in communities by giving voice to the have-nots. The mediating function of programs in this regard could be slanted toward the ICT supplier versus the demand side and, within the latter, toward the resource rich versus the resource poor, toward topical versus radical intervention. University-level programs of study in ICT application and use seldom view themselves as political activists in the local community. Indeed, there is a suspicion that not many are even sensitive to the relation between technology and human values (Kling, 2002). We are not suggesting that outreach programs should "go radical" to have legitimacy in their communities. We are arguing, however, that as the gap in ICT access continues to widen, such programs, while continuing to provide topical help, cannot be blind to the structural underpinnings of digital disparities. The discipline of urban planning offers lessons in radical practice – in the need for political activism from practitioners – that are centrally relevant to the concerns of this chapter.

In Chapter 2, we presented an extended model of active learning. Learners, we believe, respond very positively to learning activities that require the delivery of a product to an identified client. The learning activity should provide opportunities for peer learning and participation. "Real-world" organizational work usually involves cross-functional teams, where members are drawn from diverse functional areas and bring with them expertise in specific areas. Our project teams are no different. We encourage diversity of background. As was noted, the planning and design activities that comprise the project effort demand complementary abilities. Learners learn through participation in the work of their team, contributing to it in their area of expertise and learning from more knowledgeable fellow members in areas of deficiency. Drawing on task motivation models, we discussed ways to increase the motivational charge of the project.

Enhancing the micro-social relevance of project work is a central concern, one we stress in our discussion of planning and design activity with our students. Their work must be informed by the work environment – the social ecology – of the client organization. Done well, planning should provide them with a good grasp of this ecology. Design work then becomes a question of configuring a set of technical specifications that will fits well with this ecology. Working for a real client enables them to understand the criticality of micro-social relevance. They have to convince the client that their recommended design would work given the client's needs, constraints and ICT and human support resources.

In Chapter 3, we discussed the macro-social relevance of our class projects. Locating the projects in the non-profit sector in the local community was a deliberate decision and was motivated by two considerations. One, this sector, in particular the CBOs, is on the wrong side of the Digital Divide. As we have noted many times in this book, this means that the clientele served by this sector – who are among the neediest – is also denied the benefits that ICTs can bring. Two, we hoped that our students, by working on the projects, would get some sense of how "the other half lived" in the proximate community. Our classes do not examine the community's social conditions. But by thinking about technology within the specific context of an organization in the non-profit sector, our students have reported an improved understanding of the challenges such organizations struggle with every day and the social problems they are trying to address. Through the project experience, many also realize that they can help mitigate some of these challenges by their actions. It gives them a perspective – one which accommodates technical skills and social awareness – on their evolving identity as ICT professionals.

Chapter 4 summarize results from a series of evaluation studies for a course specifically designed to address the four elements of learning-in-community described in Chapter 1. Evaluation data were collected through questionnaires, interviews, surveys, and case studies in order to determine the impact of participation in these types of community-based projects on students, faculty, and non-profit agencies. The chapter concludes with a number of conclusions and recommendations related to active learning in community projects.

We described the *What* and *How* of our learning-in-community program in Chapter 5.   We traced the origins and evolution of the program, the lessons we learned en route and the adjustments we made to the organization as it grew and evolved in response both to our evolving sense of the pedagogical issues involved in community-based learning as well as to developments – notably the Urban-net – in the proximate community.

The present chapter builds on Chapter 3. Are there implications for social activism from macro-social awareness? If there are, what might they consist of? How can the socially aware ICT professional contribute to social transformation in the proximate community? How would learning-in-community programs have to change their pedagogical aims and substantive foci to better prepare students to be activists? These ideas mark a significant departure from our own practice as educators and standard models of academic outreach in that they are explicitly political in intent. We draw on the discipline of urban planning discipline to argue the need for a radical reconceptualization of ICT professional practice.

2. COMMUNITY NETWORKING REVISITED: THE QUESTION OF VALUES

Five community networking projects were analyzed in Chapter 3 from the viewpoint of user participation. Recall that the project steering committees consisted of planners, who were technical and non-technical persons representing eligible community organizations. These volunteers had drafted the project proposal and represented community interests in network design and services contracting deliberations with the telephone company (provider). Many planners were also would-be subscribers to the community network.

As reported in Chapter 3, we found that lack of access to technical knowledge was a significant impediment to participation by resource poor entities such as CBOs. These projects also brought up value conflicts. For example, in the Urban-net project, eligible organizations often had conflicting views on what the primary function of the network should be. The project featured many (organizational) stakeholders from multiple functional sectors, and these entities were diverse: some were large and relatively resource rich, others were small in size and resource poor. There were government agencies in the mix along with private organizations. Some were much better off in terms of in-house technical staff and ICT resources, while others had much less or none. Similar-size entities in the same functional sector (e.g., K-12 schools) sometimes had different needs. Not surprisingly, the network meant different things to stakeholders.

CBOs and small business entities saw the network as a high-speed Internet access ramp. Many did not have Internet access, and those that did wished to upgrade from dial-up access to broadband. Public institutions appeared more interested in using the subsidized services to meet their internal (intra-organizational) networking needs. Many already had high-speed Internet access, and meeting internal networking needs was a higher priority need for them. The CBOs were equally clear on their priorities (as noted in Chapter 3, the small business entities were so small in number that we dropped them from the analysis).. "I see no need for agencies to be linked to other agencies. It is more important to be linked to the Internet", one CBO representative argued at a design meeting. It must be emphasized that it was not an either-or issue: the Urban-net could support both types of connectivity and indeed, design specifications accommodated both options. However, the network's basic character would be different depending on the emphasis. If the design had emphasized the network-as-Internet access ramp function, the monthly subscription charges would likely have been relatively low to facilitate access by resource-poor CBOs. As it turned out, the network-for-internal connectivity function grew prominent as the design process unfolded. This of course meant higher subscription costs, which would restrict subscription to resource-rich entities like the public institutions.

Divergence in objectives confronted the steering committee with a value question: What should the defining character of the Urban-net be? Should it serve as a resource for the resource-poor or the resource-rich, or for both? Like administrative bodies in general, the committee was more competent to tackle project management and budgetary matters than value questions. Reconciling competing interpretations of network ontology and function or working through the politics of value conflict was not what many committee members expected to do as ICT planners. Consequently, such questions were either avoided or not addressed adequately in the design process. The steering committee appeared unprepared to deal with such questions.

In the end, the interpretation favored by the CBOs did not prevail. As a nominal group, they lacked clout in design meeting. They made up a relatively small market for telecommunications services. The public institutions, on the other hand, constituted a larger market and were more influential. Their willingness and capacity to pay for high-end services such as gigabit Ethernet was seen by the steering committee as "insurance" that the Urban-net project would indeed go forward as planned. Just ensuring that the project stayed on time and on budget was a daunting enough task for the committee, and they performed competently under the circumstances. However, if they had they been sensitive to the relationship between power and user participation (participation as an expression of power and as limited by power), their construal of their own role as planners, and as participants, might have expanded to include advocacy of the needs of the smaller entities. After all, the Urban-net proposal had emerged out of broad-based discussions in the community and was intended to serve a broad cross-section of needs and interests in the community.

Value questions lie at the heart of ICT design. Using as an example a digital library program called American Memory sponsored by the US Library of Congress, Kling (2002, p. 4) raises a number of critical value questions:

> But whom should the digitized collections serve?...how should American Memory depict controversial and divisive social issues that are documented in its collections, such as the social practices of Black slavery, the US governments' violation of treaties with Native Americans, and the politics of industrial pollution? Or should American Memory steer clear of controversy and provide materials that help to promote an idealized view of American social life

Such dilemmas may go unarticulated and unacknowledged if ICT development is viewed purely from a technical rational standpoint. Proponents of the technical rational view are apt to be concerned more with instrumental design criteria. The Urban-net design process unwittingly emphasized quantifiable criteria such as network performance and efficiency. Value questions – *Whom should the network serve? What should its primary function be?* – while particularly appropriate given the project's social aims, were largely absent from the discussions. Community networking projects dramatize the criticality of values-based design and are powerful when used with the idea of macro-social relevance in pedagogy.

We use the Urban-net and the other projects surveyed in Chapter 3 as examples to remind students of the criticality of value questions. As we argued in Chapter 2, students must be made mindful of the *ends* that their project work is in reference to. We remind them that concerns about ends are in the realm of values.

3. THE POLITICS OF VOICE

"Indeed, it might be argued that an exclusion of power in the consideration of participation...is something akin to describing free enterprise capitalism without talking about the profit motive" (Spiegel, 1973, p. 372, writing of citizen participation in government programs).

Why was it that some social groups were more persuasive than others in deciding what the primary function of the Urban-net would be? There were a number of reasons, but the point is, value questions can guide scrutiny of structural biases and their implications for ICT development and user participation.

Participation permits prospective users to make their voices heard in the design process and influence design outcomes. User participation is generally seen as a good thing. As one analyst remarked of citizen participation in community action programs: "The idea of citizen participation is a little like eating spinach; no one is against it in principle because it is good for you" (Arnstein, 1969, p. 216). In reality, however, user participation may not be as meaningful as proponents might wish, or it may not be possible at all due to any number of constraints and impediments. Participation in community networking projects cannot be examined without reference to the broader social setting within which the project is embedded. It must be studied in relation to the community's social structure. Structural imbalances in power can affect who participates and how effectively, and what interests get promoted and what do not. Idealist and pluralist assumptions about power distribution that seem to color most received ideas of participation in ICT projects understate their relation to the realities of structural power.

A community's social structure may be viewed as patterned relations among constituents – individuals, social groups, and organizations (Laumann, Galaskiewicz & Marsden, 1978; Nelson, Ramsey & Verner, 1960). The patterning of relations is assumed to persist over time. These entities are linked through the positions they occupy in the social network, and positions represent interests (Archer, 1995), and (differential) access to resources (Wellman, 1997). A large business organization can sway community decisions quite effectively by virtue of its location in the network; this is an example of structural power (Brint & Karabel, 1991). Any significant public project – be it community action or community networking – brings to the surface a diverse mix of more or less structurally powerful actors with different, even competing, goals and views on the project. Participation is one way that competing groups attempt to exert influence in favor of one option versus another. A structural view problematizes the idea of user participation by analyzing it in terms of the social relations, vested interests and relative power that characterize any social order.

In view of the disparities inherent in any social order, one may ask the following apropos an ICT development project with broad social aims such as the Urban-net: *What are the proper goals of participation?* And, *What is the proper role of the socially aware ICT professional?*

Participation can occur at different levels and have different goals. Arnstein (1969, p. 217) developed a typology to describe citizen participation in social programs. Her ladder of participation ranges from non-participation all the way up to where "have-not citizens obtain the majority of decision-making seats, or full managerial power". Others such as Spiegel (1973) have also proposed similar typologies. The rhetoric in these formulations is shaped by concern for the politically voiceless ("have-not citizens"), and by the recognition that redistribution of power through effective participation is a valid goal. Social programs like community action and renewal furnished the context for Arnstein and Spiegel, but we would argue that the same political goal is not misplaced in community networking projects. After all, such projects are undertaken in the public interest and purport to meet needs broadly in the locality. The have-nots must be enabled to participate meaningfully in the design of such artifacts.

The Urban-net steering committee's construal of participation was quite different from the radical interpretation advanced by the likes of Arnstein and Spiegel. Recall that the committee comprised prospective users, and represented the community's interests in design and contracting discussions with the provider. The committee, as a body, almost certainly did not consciously take a stand against a political interpretation of their role as representatives. Their approach to their assigned task was eminently reasonable, and few members would have thought of their work on the committee as anything other than the making of informed technical decisions and choices. According to the Arnstein typology, their role covered three facets: information giving, consultation, and probably partnership (with the provider's design personnel). Arnstein notes of the last: "Partnership...enables [citizens] to negotiate and engage in trade-offs with traditional power-holders" (Arnstein, 1969, p. 217). The committee saw itself as a co-operating partner in design, and the provider's design staff reciprocated this sentiment. But Arnstein's idea of partnership has an explicitly political dimension to it that was missing from the steering committees' construal of their role.

An activist construal would argue that the committee should have championed the CBOs' need for Internet connectivity using the public institutions' interest in subscribing to the Urban-net as leverage to secure an equitable outcome. Such a stance would have taken the committee well into the political domain of Arnstein's partnership modality and well beyond the information giving and consultation modes. The apolitical stance adopted (not consciously) by the committee instead ignored the well-known axiom that design work is fundamentally political: "Designers address particular audiences, not the world at large, and designed artifacts are always simultaneously both inclusive and exclusive, aimed toward particular market segments and away from others" (Brown & Duguid, 1994, p. 14). Participation occurs in a social context and is conditioned by prevailing power relations in the social order – which renders some "market segments" more influential than others.

Arguably, then, redistribution of power is a valid goal of participation. The role of the socially aware ICT professional then is to work with and represent the interests of the politically voiceless to realize equitable and socially responsible outcomes. Such a goal, and the concomitant professional role, may not always be indicated, but in the context of community network development projects with purportedly social aims, it would be hard to ignore its claims to legitimacy.

In its naivety in regard to the actual distribution of power in the social order, the Urban-net steering committee was unwittingly subscribed to pluralist-rationalist assumptions. Rose summarizes these assumptions in relation to social planning:.

> The ontological foundations of social planners seem rooted in a pluralistic assumption about the distribution of power in American society. Communities are said to be governed by interest groups which have legitimated domains of primary concern, but which can still be brought together in a rational manner to act in the "public interest" which overrides their specific concerns...planning becomes a rational process of bringing these powerful actors together around a point of mutual concern and persuading them of the import and rationality of the planners' strategy (Rose, 1973, p. 317).

And later,

> The influence of this ideology (pluralism) on rationality becomes clear when we examine its influence on planners. For them, the dictates of pluralism are unquestioned. The assumption of an altruistic rationality among the institutions of the social structure also exists a priori (Rose, 1973, p. 318)

Rose's comments were prompted by the largely unsuccessful social planning practices of the 1970s, but they do shed light on our present concerns. The reality of the Urban-net development process often ran contrary to pluralist-rationalist assumptions. The "public interest", which was explicitly acknowledged in the proposal in line with the emphasis in the program that funded the project, was not persuasive in the later design stages. Instead of the public interest overriding the self-interests of powerful entities, the latter prevailed, often at the expense of broad-based benefits.

For a number of reasons, the CBOs failed to come together and speak with one voice to secure their interests. Lack of time and human resources were often blamed: most simply did not have the flexibility in their schedules and the necessary "warm bodies" to attend the endless planning and design meetings to press their cause. This was particularly the case in the later (and crucial) stages of the project when attrition rates spiked sharply. The public institutions were better positioned with respect to both time and warm bodies, and were less affected by the long drawn-out process. The same reasons probably contributed to the CBOs' apparent inability to rise above self-interest to forge coalitions to press their concerns with the steering committee. They, as much as the resource rich entities, failed to forge a collective identity and a reflexive basis for conjoint action. Current theorizing on collective action views social capital as a resource for such action and as a necessary condition for initiating such action (Gualini, 2002). As atomized entities, CBOs lacked presence in the deliberations. Although equally un-collectivized, the resource rich entities were however a compelling presence because of their individual buying power. They could not be ignored.

4. TOWARD A RADICAL ICT PROFESSIONAL PRACTICE: LESSONS FROM URBAN PLANNING

So how can this state of affairs be changed? The value of technical assistance cannot be underestimated, and the preceding chapters stem from that conviction. Assisting

CBOs with technical know-how can be an empowering strategy in reducing the organizational version of the Digital Divide. Local institutions of higher education can be instrumental in this role. Interestingly enough, analysts of social planning and citizen empowerment recommend exactly such a role for university programs (Spiegel, 1973).

But clearly, ICT professionals can go beyond what we termed technological activism elsewhere in this book to social activism. They can do more than share their technical know-how. They can help develop and adapt strategies for political mobilization and work with social groups in using these methods effectively. They can advocate and empower the politically voiceless. In brief, they can take sides. These new roles call for an expanded construal of the learning-in-community idea itself.

Urban planning started out as a technical discipline motivated by what has been termed the rational comprehensive model. The planner was a champion of rationality and expert "knower", who used his technical expertise and objectivity to "discern and implement the public interest" (Sandercock, 1998, p. 170). This model yielded to advocacy planning. Summarizing the concerns of Paul Davidoff, an early proponent, Sandercock notes:

> Concerned that the rational model of planning was obsessed with means, he warned that the question of ends remained. He stressed the role of politics in planning. The public interest, as he saw it, was not a matter of science but politics, and he urged planners to participate in the political arena. He called for...full discussion of values and interests...He brought the question of who gets what – the distributional question which the rational model had so carefully avoided – to the foreground." (Sandercock, 1988, p. 171)

The advocacy planning model was in turn criticized for being paternalistic at best. The planner, some analysts argued (Sandercock, 1998), should find ways instead to empower the voiceless so that they represented their own interests. This led to the empowerment model.

The radical planning model, as the name suggests, is explicitly political and activist in its aims:

> Radical practices emerge from experiences with and a critique of existing unequal relations and distributions of power, opportunity and resources. The goal of these practices is to work for structural transformation of these systemic inequalities and, in the process, to empower those who have been systematically disempowered (Sandercock, 1998, p. 176)

Sandercock notes the challenge to conventional notions of professional identity posed by the notion of radical practice. As an activist, does the radical planner "cross-over" to the side of the politically weak and work essentially in "opposition to the state and corporate economy? (Sandercock, 1998, p. 178) Such concerns are complex and not easily resolvable, and we will not try to resolve them here. Our interest is in using these ideas on the evolution of urban planning to think about possible evolutionary paths for ICT planning and design practice, both in the context of community network development projects and more generally in relation to broad social problems like the Digital Divide.

(1)   As noted earlier, despite their sympathetic view of the Urban-net project's social aims, the designers (i.e. the provider's design staff) were more attuned to a technical rational view of network development. The radical ICT professional would see herself as an ally and representative of the voiceless as well as spokesperson for the broad social aims of developmental efforts such as the Urban-net. Design choices can divide and balkanize; they can have the force of implicit policy (Guthrie and Dutton, 1992). The radical ICT professional must reorient such trajectories for the public good. Technical criteria are critical in design, but so are goals such as equity, particularly when the object of design is a community network. In her new role, the new professional would use means and viewpoints considered vital in urban planning practice – the ability to question and challenge assumptions (Sandercock, 1998) – and a post-modern sensibility (Graham and Marvin, 1996), to keep the focus on the voiceless and on community-wide goals, neither of which was in evidence in later stages of the Urban-net development process.

(2)   Radical urban planning analysts argue that the politically voiceless are typically not a homogenous group but in fact comprise multiple constituents with as many "voices" (Sandercock, 1998) The new ICT professional would be sensitive to diversity in that which she champions. She would combine technical and contextualized knowledge (*in situ* knowledge (Stiglitz, 2000) of organizational milieus to empower and invite participation from diverse social groups. Given the high knowledge demands of efforts like the Urban-net, the radical professional has to continue to fulfil the role of an expert advocate in the design process. However, in terms of ideas for network use, the social groups are in charge; she would be an ally. We discussed the power of prototyping in pedagogy in Chapter 3. Prototyping can also be used to call attention to urgent social needs in the community and to influence the agenda for network uses around such needs. Prototyping, in such cases, can be used to build a social constituency around unvoiced needs; it becomes a political act. In Chapter 2 we discussed the Medicaid benefits certification prototype developed and tested by our students in the community. This prototype called attention to the needs of the elderly and infirm (who constitute a substantial portion of those applying for Medicaid benefits in the county) that the Urban-net was in a position to address but in fact did not. The elderly population in the region grew between the 1990 and 200 US Census, but they lacked a compelling voice in the design process. The new professional would use such methods to develop grassroots momentum around marginalized social groups and their interests.

Efforts at empowerment and advocacy can draw strength from ongoing social change initiatives in the community or region. The new ICT professional can help bridge such efforts. Broader initiatives such as those aimed at realizing conditions for civil society can offer important lessons for those involved in efforts aimed at equalizing access to ICTs or to their benefits. Civil society initiatives emphasize social coordination and the strengthening of horizontal relations between citizens and social groups as a way to resist pressures from the state and the marketplace (Jessop, 2000). Social groups and citizens can be effective negotiators insofar as they can function as a collective. This does not mean it must be a homogeneous entity. Rather, a functional and responsive collective would be one that is able to allocate its social and opportunity structures, and its collective voice, to issues its constituents view as relevant to their interests. The new ICT professional might use ICTs – such as community networks, Internet discussion groups – to help marginalized groups find common cause with broader social initiatives and coordinate action around it.

(3)   The new ICT professional would work with social groups to institutionalize expression of voice. How should participation be institutionalized and sustained? What can be done to ensure that participation, as a grassroots enterprise, continues to shape the Urban-net's character and function, for example? What organizational structures should be developed so that participation is ongoing and vigorous? These questions are pertinent both to bodies like the steering committee (in terms of its influence and legitimacy in the larger community) and to those it represents. The Urban-net steering committee has evolved into a standing body with fiduciary powers. The committee manages the Urban-net and sets and enforces policy on access and costs. The other half of the picture – that is, participatory structures for community residents – is much less formal and less well developed.

ICTs can be used to build horizontal relations within a community itself (and not just between social groups and social movements in the region) and can be a key element of such a participatory structure. It must be stressed, however, that support for horizontal connectivity by itself is not likely to be adequate. It would not ensure that participation will in fact occur or that it will be sustained or broad-based. Social support structures will have to develop simultaneously around ICT provisions to educate and assist residents in the active use of such features as listservs and e-mail for political purposes. The new ICT professional would work to ensure that the original purpose of participation – to register voice through broad-based engagement – is not lost sight of. Institutionalization of forms should not be confused with a stifling rigidity. As Spiegel cautioned with reference to citizen participation in social change programs:

> The problem with...institutional forms...lies in the impetus for their creation, the resources to sustain them, and once established, their capacity to foster and broaden the popular participatory base. The ultimate irony of course would be to see such institutions become another oligarchical layer that stifles broad-based community dialogue and decision-making. Then citizen participation (the institution) would have helped to kill citizen participation (the process)" (Spiegel, 1973, p. 379).

Urban planning practitioners offer lessons on power, planning, and community that are relevant to an activist construal of ICT practice. A central challenge of pragmatic social action consists of mediating between two domains (Hoch, 1996): the domain of power (control) and that of solidarity. Hoch argues for the development of urban planning methods "that can resist the encroachment of ... power relations while contributing to the practical formation of powerful democratic communities" (Hoch, p. 31). As ICTs get technologically complex and costly, as with broadband, similar methods will be needed with increasing urgency to resist the claims of structural power and assert the more socially inclusive ones of broad-based participation.

What are the implications of radical praxis for the new ICT professional's professional identity? We see the new practitioner as a socially aware pragmatist. Pragmatism, like politics itself, is the art of the possible; it is the art of what works. The Urban-net project showed that broadband ICTs demand a certain level of ICT resources and technical know-how on the subscriber's part. Without an adequate ICT infrastructure in-house, and without in-house technical staff, a subscriber would not be able to sustain use of the Urban-net. Of course, the subscriber should also be able to afford the monthly service charges. The Urban-net biased participation and subscription simply by virtue of its technological sophistication. A strategy focused exclusively on getting the resource poor onto it would probably have jeopardized the project because few would have been able to afford it. The steering committee was justified, up to a point, in pointing out that interest in the Urban-net from resource rich entities in the community was vital for its realization.

However, creative ideas were proposed in the steering committee to protect the interests of the resource poor while catering to the needs of the resource rich. But these were not pursued. A socially aware pragmatist would have actively championed such ideas.

How would we modify learning-in-community for training the radical practitioner? The social content of our present courses would probably have to be strengthened with ideas and viewpoints from the social sciences, specifically from social studies of technology development and use. Urban planning methods focused on dialogue and empowerment are likely to be useful. Hands-on project work in the local community would continue to be a valuable learning tool, with a significant place in the curriculum given to structured reflection on the experience. Hands-on learning would be supplemented with detailed analysis of case studies of community networking and other developmental initiatives with broad social implications, such as the building of a shopping mall or an inter-state highway. Whose interests are served by such initiatives, and whose are ignored? Case studies of popular resistance to such initiatives would be valuable as well.

REFERENCES

Adler, M.W. (1994). Experiential Education: A View from the Top. Paper presented at *the Annual Meeting of the American Political Science Association,* New York: Sept. 1-4, 1994, ERIC Clearinghouse. (ED 383 600).

Arnstein, S. R. (1969). Ladder of citizen participation. *Journal of the American Institute of Planners, 35* (4), 216-224.

Attewell, P. (1992). Technology diffusion and organizational learning: The case of business computing. *Organization Science, 3* (1), 1-19.

Brint, S. & Karabel, J. (1991). Institutional Origins and Transformations: The Case of American Community Colleges. In W.W. Powell and P. J. DiMaggio (Eds.,), *The New Institutionalism in Organizational Analysis* (pp. 143-163). Chicago, IL: University of Chicago Press.

Brown, J.S., & Duguid, P. (1994). Borderline issues: Social and material aspects of design. *Human-Computer Interaction, 9,* 3-36.

Buchanan, R. (1995). Wicked problems in design thinking. In V. Margolin and R. Buchanan (Eds.,) *The idea of design: A Design Issues reader* (pp. 3-20). Cambridge, MA: MIT Press.

Calhoun, C. (1998). Community without Propinquity Revisited: Communications Technology and the Transformation of the Urban Public Sphere. *Sociological Inquiry, 68* (3), 373-397.

Coyne, R. (1995). *Designing information technology in the postmodern age: From method to metaphor.* Cambridge, MA: MIT Press.

Cooper, M. N. (2002). Does the Digital Divide still exist? Bush Administration shrugs, but evidence says "Yes". In *The success and failure of the 1996 Telecommunications Act* (pp.223-249). Center for Reflective Community Practice, MIT, and the Leadership Conference Education Fund.

Dewey, J. (1927). *The Public and its Problems.* Athens. OH: Ohio University Press.

Evaluation Report (2001). New York State Advanced Telecommunication Project. Prepared by Magi Educational Consulting, New York.

Findeli, A. (1995). Moholy-Nagy' design pedagogy in Chicago (1937-46). In V. Margolin and R. Buchanan (Eds.,), *The idea of design: A Design Issues reader* (pp. 29-43). Cambridge, MA: MIT Press.

Graham, S., & Marvin, S. (1996). *Telecommunications and the city: Electronic spaces, Urban places.* London, UK: Routledge.

Greater Springfield Health Access Project. (2002). Proposal prepared by the Department of Health and Human Services. Springfield, MA.

Greenbaum, J., & Halskov Madsen, K. (1993). Small changes: Starting a participatory design process by giving participants a voice. In D. Schuler & A. Namioka (Eds.), *Participatory Design: Principles and Practices* (pp. 289-298). Hillsdale, NJ: Lawrence Erlbaum Associates.

Gronbaek, K., Grudin, J., Bodker, S., and Bannon, L. (1993). Achieving cooperative system design: Shifting from a product to a process focus. In D. Schuler & A. Namioka (Eds.*), Participatory Design: Principles and Practices* (pp. 79-97). Hillsdale, NJ: Lawrence Erlbaum Associates.

Gronbaek, K., Kyng, M., and Mogensen, P. (1997). Toward a cooperative experimental system development approach. In M. Kyng & L. Mathiassen (Eds.), *Computers and Design in Context* (pp. 201-238). Cambridge, MA: MIT Press.

119

Guthrie, K., and Dutton, W. (1992). The politics of citizen access technology: The development of public information utilities in four cities. *Policy Studies Journal, 20* (4), 574-597.

Gualini, E. (2002). Institutional capacity building as an issue of collective action and institutionalization: Some theoretical remarks. In G. Cars, P. Healey, A. Madanipour and C. De Magalhaes (Eds.,), *Urban governance, institutional capacity and social milieux* (pp. 29-44). Aldershot, UK: Ashgate.

Hackman, J. R. & Oldham,, G. R. (1980). *Work Redesign.* Reading. MA: Addison-Wesley.

Hoch, C. (1996). A pragmatic inquiry about planning and power. In S. J. Mandelbaum, L. Mazza., and R. W. Burchell (Eds.)., *Explorations in planning theory.* (pp.30-44). New Brunswick, NJ: Rutgers University Press.

Ishida, T (2000). Understanding digital cities. In T. Ishida and K. Isbister (Eds.)., *Digital Cities: Technologies, experiences and future perspectives* (pp. 246-260). Berlin, Germany: Springer-Verlag.

Keller, J.M. (1987). Development and use of the ARCS model of motivational design. *Journal of Instructional Development,* 10 (3), 2-10.

Kensing, F., & Munk-Madsen, A. (1993). PD: Structure in the toolbox. *Communications of the ACM, 36*(6), 78-85 (June 1993).

Kling, R., & Scacchi, W. (1982). The Web of Computing: Computer Technology as Social Organization. *Advances in Computers,* 21, 1-90.

Kling, R. (2002). *Critical professional discourses about information and communications technologies and social life in the US.* Bloomington, IN: Center for Social Informatics, Indiana University.

Kling, R., Crawford, H., Rosenbaum, H., Sawyer, S., & Weisband, S. (2000). *Learning from social informatics: Information and communication technologies in human context.* Bloomington, IN: Center for Social Informatics, Indiana University.

Kolb, D.A. (1984). *Experiential learning: experience as the source of learning and development.* Englewood Cliffs, NJ: Prentice-Hall.

Kruglanski, A.W. (1989). *Lay epistemic and human knowledge: Cognitive and motivational bases.* New York: Plenum.

Laumann, E.O., Galaskiewicz, J. & Marsden, P.V. (1978). Community structure as interorganizational linkages. *Annual Review of Sociology,* 4, 455-484.

Lave, J. (1993). Introduction. In S. Chaiklin & J. Lave (Eds.,), Understanding practice: *Perspectives on activity and context.* New York, NY: Cambridge University Press.

Lave, J., & Wenger, E. (1991). *Situated Learning: Legitimate Peripheral Participation.* Cambridge, MA: Cambridge University Press.

Lewin, K. (1951). *Field theory in social sciences.* New York, NY: Harper & Row.

Margolin, V. (1995). Expanding the boundaries of design: The product environment and the new user. In V. Margolin and R. Buchanan (Eds.,), *The idea of design: A Design Issues reader* (pp. 275-280). Cambridge, MA: MIT Press.

Nelson, L., Ramsey, C. & Verner, C. (1960). *Community structure and change.* New York, NY: Macmillan.

Papert, S. (1990). Introduction: Constructionist learning. In I. Harel (Ed.), *Constructionist learning: A fifth anniversary collection of papers.* Cambridge, MA: MIT Media Laboratory.

Piaget, J. 1970. *Genetic epistemology.* New York, NY: Columbia University Press.

Program First Round RFP, (1996). New York State Advanced Telecommunications Project.

Public Utility Law Project and NY State Community Action Association. (2000). Comments filed with the Public Service Commission.

Sandercock, L. (1998). The death of modernist planning: Radical praxis for a post-modern age. In M. Douglass and J. Friedmann (Eds.,) , *Cities for citizens: Planning and the rise of civil society in a global age* (163-184). Chichester, UK: John Wiley.

Serra, A. (2000). Next Generation Community Networking: Futures for Digital Cities. In T. Ishida and K. Isbister (Eds.)., *Digital Cities: Technologies, experiences and future perspectives* (pp. 45-57). Berlin, Germany: Springer-Verlag.

Schein, E.H. & Kommers, D.W. (1972). *Professional Education.* New York, NY: McGraw-Hill.

Schon, D. A., (1983). *The Reflective Practitioner.* New York, NY: Basic Books.

Shaw, A., & Shaw, M. (1999). Social empowerment through community networks. In D.A. Schon, B. Sanyal, and W.J. Mitchell (Eds.,), *High technology and low-income communities: Prospects for the positive use of advanced information technology* (pp. 317-335). Cambridge, MA: MIT Press.

Small, R.V., & Venkatesh, M. (1998). Linking technology training and community service: An active learning approach. In M. Khosrowpur (Ed.), Effective utilization and management of emerging information technologies. *Proceedings of the 1998 Information Resources Management Association international Conference*, Boston, MA, May 17-20. Hershey, PA: Idea Group Publishing.

Spiegel, H.B.C (1973). Citizen participation in federal programs: A review. In R.L. Warren (Ed.), *Perspectives on the American community* (pp 365-389). Chicago, IL: Rand McNally.

Stanton, T.K. (1987). Liberal Arts, Experiential Learning and Public Service: Necessary Ingredients for Socially Responsible Undergraduate Education. *Paper presented at the 16th Annual Conference of the National Society for Internships and Experiential Education,* Oct. 15, 1987.

Stewart, D.W. (1982). The Diffusion of Innovations: A Review of Research and Theory with Implications for Computer Technology. Paper presented at *the Annual Convention of the American Psychological Association* (Washington, DC, August 1982). (ERIC NO: ED224480)

Stiglitz, J. (2000). Scan globally, reinvent locally. Knowledge infrastructure and the localization of knowledge. In D. Stone (Ed.), *Banking on knowledge: The genesis of the global development network* (pp. 24-43). London, UK: Routledge.

Rose, S.M. (1973). The transformation of community action. In R.L. Warren (Ed.), *Perspectives on the American community* (pp. 311-320). Chicago, IL: Rand McNally.

Thoresen, K. (1993). Principles in practice: Two cases of situated participatory design. In D. Schuler & A. Namioka (Eds.), *Participatory Design: Principles and Practices* (pp. 271-289). Hillsdale, NJ: Lawrence Erlbaum Associates.

Tornatzky, L.G. (1983). Research on Innovation: Stretching the Limits of the Discipline. Paper presented at *the Annual Convention of the American Psychological Association* (Anaheim, CA, August 26-30, 1983). (ERIC NO: ED237861)

US Department of Commerce National Telecommunications and Information Administration, (1999). Falling through the Net III: Defining the Digital Divide. Full report.

Wagemans, L. & Dochy, F. (1991). Principles in the use of experiential learning as a source of prior knowledge. *Distance Education,* 12 (1), 85-108.

Wellman, B. (1997). Structural analysis: From method and metaphor to theory and substance. In B. Wellman and S.D. Berkowitz (Eds.,), *Social structures: A network approach* (pp. 19-61). Greenwich, CT: JAI Press.